# Dark Lore

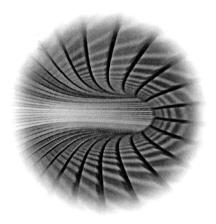

Daily Grail Publishing

**Darklore Volume 7**
Copyright © 2012 by Greg Taylor (Editor)

Contributing authors retain ownership and all rights to their individual pieces.

All rights reserved. No part of this book may be reproduced, stored, or transmitted in any form without permission in writing from the publisher, except by a reviewer who may quote brief passages for review purposes.

ISBN: 978-0-9874224-0-8

Daily Grail Publishing
Brisbane, Australia
userhelp@dailygrail.com
www.dailygrail.com

# Contents

| | |
|---|---|
| Introduction | 7 |
| Mushrooms in Wonderland • *Mike Jay* | 9 |
| Dirt Roads to Dreamland • *Blair MacKenzie Blake* | 23 |
| The Uninvited • *Greg Taylor* | 45 |
| The Executable Dreamtime • *Mark Pesce* | 71 |
| Herne the Hunter • *Richard Andrews* | 89 |
| From Operation Mindf**k to The White Room • *J.M.R. Higgs* | 105 |
| Origin of the Space Gods • *Jason Colavito* | 129 |
| House of the Swastika • *Theo Paijmans* | 151 |
| The Starry Wisdom • *Paolo Sammut* | 169 |
| Killing Slenderman • *Ian 'Cat' Vincent* | 185 |
| The Enigmatic Doctor Dee • *Robert M. Schoch* | 211 |
| Science and Imagination • *Ray Grasse* | 241 |
| Endnotes and Sources | 253 |

"The beauties of the solid and material universe are but a part of the rich spectrum of existence. The one-tenth of an iceberg that is visible above the tideline of reality. Matter is that part of being that has crystallised, where the mind's light has petrified to concrete substance."

*– Alan Moore ('Promethea')*

If you would like to be notified of future releases of *Darklore*, please send an email to darklore@dailygrail.com. Please be assured your contact details will not be used for any other purpose.

# Editor's Introduction

In every *Darklore* release a few major themes present themselves, running like a thread throughout the volume. I don't plan for this to happen, but I do notice them as I work through the editing and typesetting of the articles. In this latest release the idea that appears to be presenting itself within the next 260 pages is, funnily enough, the ways in which ideas and the imagination manifest themselves in physical reality.

In his fantastic essay "The Executable Dreamtime", Mark Pesce not only explains how humans are removed from direct perception of 'reality' by the mediation of language and symbols, but also points out that language can be imposed upon reality to effect change. "To speak and be heard," Mark says, "means that you are sending your will out onto the world around you, changing the definition of reality for all those who hear you." And in reading the thoughts in Mark's essay regarding our circular relationship with the technology we 'imagine' into the world, I was reminded of the words of Terence McKenna, who noted the human ability to take in matter that has a low degree of organization and "put it through mental filters, and… extrude jewelry, gospels, space shuttles… We are like coral animals embedded in a technological reef of extruded psychic objects."

The title of Ray Grasse's essay, "Science and Imagination", hints that it touches on similar themes; and Ray echoes both Mark Pesce and Terence McKenna in noting that the progress of science "has been as much a reflection of inner, psychological exploration, projected out onto the world, as it is one of external discovery." And in other essays, Cat Vincent, Robert Schoch and Paolo Sammut all discuss well-known magical practitioners and the willing of thoughts into reality. Many ideas to ruminate on, but also much fun to be had, so dig in and enjoy the full course of *Darklore Volume 7*!

# Mushrooms in Wonderland

Was Victorian fairy art and lore inspired by actual experiences with mind-altering fungi?

by *Mike Jay*

The first well-documented hallucinogenic mushroom experience in Britain took place in London's Green Park on 3 October 1799. Like many such experiences before and since, it was accidental. A man subsequently identified only as 'J.S.' was in the habit of gathering small field mushrooms from the park on autumn mornings, and cooking them up into a breakfast broth for his wife and young family. But this particular morning, an hour after they had finished eating, the world began to turn very strange. J.S. found black spots and odd flashes of colour bursting across his vision; he became disorientated, and had difficulty in standing and moving around. His family were complaining of stomach cramps and cold, numb extremities. The notion of poisonous toadstools leapt to his mind, and he staggered out into the streets to seek help. but within a hundred yards he had forgotten where he was going, or why, and was found wandering about in a confused state.

By chance, a doctor named Everard Brande happened to be passing through this insalubrious part of town, and he was summoned to treat J.S. and his family. The scene that he discovered was so bizarre and unfamiliar that he would write it up at length and publish it in *The Medical and Physical Journal* later that year. The family's symptoms were rising and falling in giddy waves, their pupils dilated, their pulses and breathing becoming fluttering and laboured, then returning to normal before accelerating into another crisis. They were all fixated on the fear that they were dying, except for the youngest, the eight-year-old Edward S., whose symptoms were the strangest of all. He had eaten a large portion of the mushrooms and was "attacked with fits of immoderate laughter" which his parents' threats could not subdue. He seemed to have been transported into another world, from which he would only return under duress to speak nonsense: "when roused and interrogated as to it, he answered indifferently, yes or no, as he did to every other question, evidently without any relation to what was asked".

Dr. Everard Brande would diagnose the family's condition as the "deleterious effects of a very common species of agaric [mushroom], not hitherto suspected to be poisonous". Today, we can be more specific: this was clearly intoxication by Liberty Caps (*Psilocybe semilanceata*), the 'magic mushrooms' which grow plentifully across the hills, moors, commons, golf courses and playing fields of Britain every autumn. But though Dr. Brande's account of the J.S. family's trip would not be forgotten, and would continue to be cited in Victorian drug literature for decades, the nineteenth century would come and go without any conclusive identification of the Liberty Cap as the species in question. In fact, it would not be until Albert Hoffman, the discoverer of LSD, turned his attention to hallucinogenic mushrooms in the 1950s that the botanical identity of these and other mushrooms containing psilocybin, LSD's chemical cousin, would be confirmed.

But if they were obscure to Victorian science, there was another tradition which would appear to explore the ability of certain mushrooms to whisk humans off to another world: Victorian fairy lore. Over the nineteenth century, a vast body of art and literature would connect mushrooms and toadstools with elves, pixies, hollow hills and the unwitting transport of subjects to fairyland, a world of shifting perspectives and dimensions seething with elemental spirits. Is it possible that the Victorian fairy tradition, underneath its twee and bourgeois exterior, operated as a conduit for a hidden world of homegrown psychedelia, parallel perhaps to the ancient shamanic and ritual uses of similar mushrooms in the New World? Were the authors of such otherworld narratives – *Alice in Wonderland*, for example – aware of the powers of certain mushrooms to lead unsuspecting visitors to enchanted lands? Were they, perhaps, even writing from personal experience?

## Rediscovering Lost Magic

The J.S. family's trip in 1799 is a useful jumping-off point for such enquiries, because it establishes several basic facts. First – and contrary to the opinion of some recent American scholars – British (and European) magic mushrooms are not a recent arrival from the New World, but were part of our indigenous flora at least two hundred years ago. Second, the species in question was unknown at the time, at least to science. Third, its hallucinogenic effects were unfamiliar, perhaps even unheard of – certainly unprecedented enough for a London doctor to feel the need to draw them to the attention of his medical colleagues.

In other scholarly contexts, though, the mind-altering effects of certain plants were already familiar. Through classical sources like *The Golden Ass*, the idea of witches' potions which transformed their subjects was an inheritance from antiquity. The pharmacopeia and *materia medica* of doctors and herbalists had long included the drug effects of common plants like belladonna and opium poppies, though mushrooms had featured in them rarely. The eighteenth century had turned up several more exotic examples from distant cultures: Russian explorers describing the use of fly agaric mushrooms in Siberia, Captain Cook observing the *kava-kava* ritual in Polynesia. In 1762 Carl Linnaeus, the great taxonomist and father of modern botany, had compiled the first ever list of intoxicating plants: his monograph, entitled *Inebriantia*, had included opium, cannabis, datura, henbane and tobacco. Slowly, the study of such plants was emerging from the margins and tall tales of classical studies, ethnography, folklore and medicine and becoming a subject in its own right.

It was as part of this same interest that European fairy lore was also being assembled by a new generation of amateur folklore collectors such as the Brothers Grimm, who realised that the inexorable drift of peasant populations from country to city was beginning

*Amanita muscaria*, the 'Fly Agaric'

to dismantle centuries of folk stories, songs and oral histories. The Victorian fairy tradition, as it emerged, would be imbued with this new sensibility which rendered rustic traditions no longer coarse, backward and primitive but picturesque and semi-sacred, an escape from the austerity of industrial living into an ancient, often pagan otherworld. Under the guise of 'innocence', sensual and erotic themes could be explored with a boldness not permitted in more realistic genres, and the muddy and impoverished countryside could be re-enchanted with imagery drawn from the classical and arabesque. Within this process, the lore of plants and flowers was carefully curated and woven into supernatural tapestries of flower-fairies and enchanted woods; and within this imaginal world of plants, mushrooms and toadstools began popping up all over. Fairy rings and toadstool-dwelling elves were recycled through a pictorial culture of motif and decoration until they became emblematic of fairyland itself.

This was a quiet but substantial image makeover for Britain's fungi. Previously, in herbals and medical texts, they had been largely shunned, associated with dung-heaps and poison; in Romantic poetry the smell of death had still clung to them ("fungous brood/coloured like a corpse's cheek", as Keats put it). Now, a new generation of folklorists began to wax lyrical about them, including Thomas Keightley, whose *The Fairy Mythology* (1850) was perhaps the most influential text on the fictional fairy tradition. Keightley gives Welsh and Gaelic examples of traditional names for fungi which invoke elves and Puck, and at one point wonders if such names refer to "those pretty small delicate fungi, with their conical heads, which are named Fairy-mushrooms in Ireland, where they grow so plentifully". This description is a very good match for the Liberty Cap, though Keightley seems unaware of its hallucinogenic properties; he was struck simply by the pixie-cap shape of its head. In Ireland, the Gaelic slang for mushrooms is 'pookies', which Keightley associated with the elemental nature spirit Pooka (hence Puck); it's a slang term which persists in Irish drug culture today, although evidence for a pre-modern Gaelic magic mushroom culture remains elusive.

But despite the presence of Liberty Caps in Britain, and their occasional tentative identification with nature spirits, it was a different mushroom which would become the immediately recognisable symbol for fairyland: the unmistakable red-and-white fly agaric (*Amanita muscaria*), which remains the classic 'fairy fungus' to this day in modern survivals of the Victorian fairy cult such as garden gnomes. The fly agaric is the most spectacular of the generally spectacular agaric family, which also includes the tawny Panther Cap (*Amanita pantherina*) and the prodigiously poisonous Death Cap (*Amanita phalloides*). The other salient fact about it is that it, too, is psychoactive. Unlike the Liberty Cap, which delivers psilocybin in fairly standard doses, the fly agaric contains an unpredictable mixture of alkaloids – muscarine, muscimol, ibotenic acid – which produce a cocktail of effects including general wooziness and disorientation, drooling, sweats, numbness in the lips and extremities, nausea, muscle twitches, sleep and a vague, often retrospective sense of liminal consciousness and waking dreams.

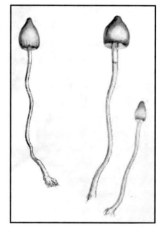

'Liberty Cap'

Unlike the Liberty Cap, the fly agaric was hard to ignore or misidentify; its effects had long been known, though they had been classed simply as poisonous. Its name was derived from its ability to kill flies, and it was otherwise generally avoided. It was the aura of livid beauty and danger which it carried, rather than its chemistry, which made it such a popular fairy motif. Yet at the same time its psychic effects were coming to be understood, not from any tradition of its use in Britain, but from the recent discovery of its visionary role among the remote peoples of Siberia.

Victorian era New Years greeting card showing *Amanita muscaria* and a gnome

Sporadically through the eighteenth century, Swedish colonels and Russian explorers had returned from Siberia with tall tales of shamans, spirit possession and self-poisoning with brightly-coloured toadstools, but it was a Polish traveller named Joseph Kopék who, in 1837, was the first to write an account of his own experience with the fly agaric. Kopék had been living in Kamchatka for two years years when he was taken ill with a fever and was told by a local of a 'miraculous' mushroom which would cure him. He ate half a fly agaric, and fell into a vivid fever dream. "As though magnetised", he was drawn through "the most attractive gardens where only pleasure and beauty seemed to rule"; beautiful women dressed in white fed him with fruits, berries and flowers.

He woke after a long and healing sleep and took a second, stronger dose, which precipitated him back into sleep and the sense of an epic voyage into other worlds, teeming with "things which I would never imagine even in my thoughts". He relived swathes of his childhood, re-encountered friends from throughout his life, and even predicted the future at length with such confidence that a priest was summoned to witness. He concluded with a challenge to science: "If someone can prove that both the effect and the influence of the mushroom are non-existent, then I shall stop being defender of the miraculous mushroom of Kamchatka".

Kopék's toadstool epiphany was widely reported, and it began a fashion for re-examining elements of European folklore and culture and interpolating fly agaric intoxication into odd corners of myth and tradition. Perhaps the best example of this is the notion that the berserkers, the Viking shock troops of the 8th to 10th centuries, drank a fly agaric potion before going into battle and fighting like men possessed. This is regularly asserted as fact not only among mushroom and Viking aficionados but also in text-books and encyclopaedias; nevertheless, it's almost certainly a creation of the nineteenth century. There's no reference to fly agaric, or indeed to any exotic plant stimulants, in the sagas or eddas: the notion of mushroom-intoxicated berserker warriors was first suggested by the Swedish professor Samuel Ödman in his *Attempt to Explain the Berserk-Raging of Ancient Nordic Warriors through Natural History* (1784), which was simply speculation based on eighteenth-century Siberian accounts. By the end of the nineteenth century scholars like the Norwegian botanist Frederik Christian Schübeler had taken Ödman's suggestion as proof. The rest is history – or, more likely, urban myth.

Thus, by the mid nineteenth century, the fly agaric had not only become an instantly recognisable fairyland motif but had also, and separately, been established as a portal to the land of dreams, and written into European folklore from exotic sources. This doesn't invalidate the claim that mushrooms in fairy literature represent the concealed or half-forgotten knowledge of their hallucinogenic properties – it's impossible to disprove such a negative – but it does show how fairy art and literature could have evolved without any such knowledge. Some may well have been directly drug-inspired –

an obvious candidate would be John Anster Fitzgerald's phantasmic paintings of dreaming subjects surrounted by distended, otherdimensional goblin creatures – but the drug in question is far more likely to have been opium, the omnipresent Victorian panacea.

## ONE SIDE WILL MAKE YOU TALLER

But there is a case where we can be more specific. The most famous and frequently-debated conjunction of fungi, psychedelia and fairy-lore is the array of mushrooms and hallucinatory potions, mindbending and shapeshifting motifs in *Alice's Adventures in Wonderland* (1865). Do Alice's adventures represent first-hand knowledge of the hallucinogenic effects of mushrooms? And, if not, how were they assembled without it?

The facts in the case could hardly be better known. Alice, down the rabbit hole, meets a blue caterpillar sitting on a mushroom, which tells her in a "languid, sleepy voice" that the mushroom is the key to navigating through her strange journey: "one side will make you grow taller, the other side will make you grow shorter". Alice takes a chunk from each side of the mushroom, and begins a series of vertiginous transformations of size, shooting up into the clouds before learning to maintain her normal size by eating alternate bites. Throughout the rest of the book she continues to take the mushroom: entering the house of the duchess, approaching the domain of the march hare and, climactically, before entering the hidden garden with the golden key.

Since the 1960s all this has frequently been read as an initiatic work of drug literature, an esoteric guide to the other worlds opened up by mushrooms and other psychedelics – most memorably, perhaps, in Jefferson Airplane's psychedelic anthem *White Rabbit* (1967), which conjures Alice's journey as a path of self-discovery where the stale advice of parents is transcended by the guidance

received from within by 'feeding your head'. By and large, this reading has provoked outrage and disgust among Lewis Carroll scholars, who seem to regard his critics' accusations of paedophilia as inoffensive by comparison.

But there's plenty of evidence that medication and unusual states of consciousness exercised a profound fascination for Carroll, and he read about them voraciously. His interest was spurred by his own delicate health – insomnia and frequent migraines – which he treated with homeopathic remedies, including many derived from psychoactive plants like aconite and belladonna. His library included several books on homeopathy as well as standard texts on mind-altering drugs like W.B.Carpenter's *Mental Physiology* (1874) and F.E.Anstie's influential compendium *Stimulants and Narcotics* (1864). He was greatly intrigued by the epileptic seizure of an Oxford student at which he was present, and visited St.Bartholemew's Hospital in London in order to witness chloroform anaesthesia.

Nevertheless, it seems that Alice's mind-expanding journeys owed little to the actual drug experiences of their author. Although Carroll – in everyday life, of course, the Reverend Charles Dodgson – was a moderate drinker and, to judge by his library, opposed to alcohol prohibition, he had a strong dislike of tobacco smoking and wrote sceptically in his letters about the pervasive presence in syrups and soothing tonics of powerful narcotics like opium – the "medicine so dexterously, but ineffectually, concealed in the jam of our early childhood". In an era where few embarked on personal drug exploration without both robust health and a compelling reason, he remains a very unlikely self-experimenter.

But it seems we can offer a more precise account. The scholar Michael Carmichael has demonstrated that, a few days before writing Alice, Carroll made his only ever visit to the Bodleian library, where a copy of Mordecai Cooke's recently-published drug survey *The Seven Sisters of Sleep* (1860) had been deposited. The Bodleian copy of this book still has most of its pages uncut, with the notable exception of the contents page and the chapter on the fly agaric, entitled 'The Exile of Siberia'. Carroll was particularly interested in all things Russian: in fact, Russia was the only country he ever visited outside Britain. And, as Carmichael puts it, "Dodgson would have been immediately attracted to Cooke's *Seven Sisters of Sleep* for two more obvious reasons: he had seven sisters and he was a lifelong insomniac".

Cooke's chapter on fly agaric is, like the rest of *Seven Sisters,* a useful compendium of the drug lore and anecdotes which were familiar to the Victorians. It recalls Dr.Everard Brande's account of the J.S. family; it rounds up the various Siberian accounts of fly agaric; it also focuses on precisely the effects of mushroom intoxication which Carroll wove into Alice's adventures. "Erroneous impressions of size and distance are common occurrences", Cooke records of the fly agaric. "A straw lying in the road becomes a formidable object, to overcome which, a leap is taken sufficient to clear a barrel of ale, or the prostrate trunk of a British oak".

Whether or not Carroll read this actual copy, it seems very likely that the properties of the mushroom in Alice were based on his encounter with Siberian fly agaric reportage rather than any hidden British tradition of its use, let alone the author's own. If so, he was neither the secret drug initiate that has been claimed, nor the Victorian gentleman entirely innocent of the arcane knowledge of drugs subsequently imputed to him. In this sense, Alice's otherworld experiences seem to hover, like much of Victorian fairy literature and fantasy, in a borderland between naïve innocence of such drugs and knowing references to them.

**Mike Jay's** *Emperors of Dreams: Drugs in the Nineteenth Century* was republished last year in a fully revised edition. A revised edition of *The Influencing Machine: James Tilly Matthews and the Air Loom* appeared this year from Strange Attractor Press.

# DIRT ROADS TO dreamland

## Fifty-One Trips to Area 51

by *Blair MacKenzie Blake*

It was only moments after we started climbing from the trailhead that I began to sense that something wasn't quite right. With the beam of my flashlight illuminating a rocky ridge studded with Joshua trees, I noticed that all traces of the reflective metallic gold tape that I had at one time wrapped around their spiky gnarled limbs in order to mark the route had been removed. Even more worrisome was the absence of orange wooden posts that marked the border of the Restricted Zone – restricted, meaning that if violated, the intruder surrendered all of his/her civil liberties. In fact, such was the level of intimidation that signs warned potential trespassers "Use of Deadly Force Authorized." Already huffing during the most strenuous part of the 45 minute hike on this bitter cold April's night in the Nevada high desert, as I paused to get my bearings my eager friend (drummer Danny Carey of the prog-metal band, Tool) continued to slowly make his way up the steep sandy slope, negotiating sharp rocks, creosote bush scrub, and dried cow patties. Searching again with my flashlight but unable to locate any gold banded Joshuas, suddenly, from seemingly out of nowhere, a deep voice calmly said, "Gentlemen, you're going to jail."

Flinching, I turned to see a man dressed in camouflage fatigues wearing night-vision goggles who was pointing an M-16 at us. Although it had been utterly silent seconds before, he had managed to sneak up undetected, and was now merely a few feet away. Before we could react, two white Jeep Cherokees crowned with light bars pulled up and flooded the ridgeline with powerful spotlights. In the crunch of trampled sage, several more security personnel approached brandishing automatic weapons. Our steep trek along the perimeter of the secret military installation, listed on old government maps as AREA 51, had abruptly come to an end. "You don't look like Iraqi spies!" one of them joked. Nevertheless, we were forced to lie on the scruffy desert floor while they searched our backpacks, removing a spotting scope, but, fortunately, no cameras. With my face pressed against the hard alkaline soil, I thought about replying to the "camou-dude" that with the Open Skies Treaty having been signed in 1992, it was (or soon would be) perfectly legal for anyone – including Iraqi spies – to photograph the base. Anyone, so it seemed, except for American citizens whose tax dollars had paid for the place.

Rather than shoot us on the spot and leave our bodies for the coyotes, we were informed that the Lincoln County sheriff had been dispatched to take us to jail. It was at this point that I found out that Danny and I were the first civilians to have fallen victim of the Air Force's most recent expansion of the base's perimeter – 3972 additional acres of public land that was seized on April 10, 1995. This latest acquisition also included two unobstructed vantage points (somehow overlooked during an earlier government land-grab) of

A marked Joshua Tree (photo by Blair MacKenzie Blake)

the remote test facility whose cloaked existence attracted curiosity seekers hoping to glimpse its highly classified activities – whether it be unconventional black-budget aircraft or the physics-defying sci-fi exotica that are rumored to be flown there.

We never did go to any damp pokey that night. Instead, we were each issued citations for $600.00 dollars and given papers warning us not to reenter the military reservation by order of the "Installation Commander."

## "Freedom Ridge"

Of course we did return…many times. In fact, I had actually viewed the 'non-existent' base on numerous occasions beginning back in 1989, before Area 51 spawned a cottage industry and became a ufological and conspiracy theory cliché. In those early days the intimidation tactics were even more extreme, with the most menacing feature being a modified Black Hawk helicopter that skimmed the sparsely-forested ridges, lowering its landing skids while sandblasting any would-be snoopers with its noisy rotor downwash.

Each time we made the hike to the (then) legal overlooks, we were shadowed by the anonymous security forces. If we didn't make our presence known by tripping buried roadside sensors, a series of strange chrome spheres suspended on tall poles (believed to be motion detectors with ammonia sensors) surely did. Add to this formidable security (in the buffer zone of the buffer zone!), motion and thermal alarms disguised as Joshua trees and high-powered range-tracking video cameras mounted on tripods (today this surveillance is probably done by miniature spy drones). Upon reaching the viewpoints of the playa below – my favorite being a promontory called "Freedom Ridge" (named by an intrepid Area 51 researcher) – in partial moonlight the secret base appeared in sharp relief against the craggy outlines of jumbled hills. Amid the vivid blues and reds of runway beacons, the Air Force's "remote operating location" was revealed to be an extensive complex, complete with large hangars, a control tower, radar domes, fuel-tank farms, satellite dishes and support facilities. Yet, one had to wonder if some of these more conventional features were merely a façade for the more ingeniously concealed structures and/or subsurface installations that house secret experimental technology. If certain shocking allegations are to be believed, some of this might even include aeroforms that defy description. According to one insider: "To compare them to the SR-71 [spyplane] would be like comparing Leonardo da Vinci's parachute design to the space shuttle." Indeed, on one occasion while perched atop the ridge, looking for something 'black' with our optics and scanners, a static-laden voice on a military channel warned someone at the base to "be advised that there are currently people in the bleachers." Had our presence on that night caused certain scheduled operations to be canceled? If so, one hopes they weren't, to quote another insider, "things so far beyond the comprehension of the average aviation authority as to be really alien to our way of thinking."

The author, at 'Freedom Ridge' (photo by G.Edward Giunca)

## Supersonic Espionage

With the growing popularity of America's most famous secret base, numerous researchers have sought to divulge its redacted history.

From declassified documents and the firsthand testimony of former pilots, engineers, scientists, and even the occasional black-world spook, many of its mysterious activities and covert operations are no longer secret (even if Area 51 still officially doesn't exist).

Located 100 miles north of Las Vegas on a dry lakebed ringed by the parched Groom Range, Area 51, also known as "Paradise Ranch", "Dreamland", and "Watertown Strip", was conceived by the CIA in the mid-fifties. As a product of Cold War paranoia, the barren landscape was transformed into the original testing grounds of long-range reconnaissance platforms developed under intense secrecy. These CIA (and later Air Force) spy-planes included the U2, Oxcart A-12, SR-71 Blackbird, and F-117 Stealth Fighter. Perhaps even more suppressed than these classified programs were extreme bio-hazards as a result of both earlier atomic mishaps and the later burning of toxic, radar-absorbing (Stealth) composites in large open

Area 51/Groom Lake Photograph (Credit: Doc Searls, CCAG licence)

pits. Though originally covered up, it has recently been revealed that also tested (and crashed) were captured foreign advanced fighter jets that were surreptitiously smuggled into the base. However, in 1989, one whistleblower claimed that something being tested near Area 51 qualified as being *truly* foreign.

## A Higher Form of Hungarian

Viewers who tuned into a special report on KLAS-TV (Las Vegas) in the spring of 1989 were no doubt left to wonder as a figure in black silhouette claimed that he had recently worked on a project to reverse engineer the propulsion system of a captured alien spacecraft, at a top secret facility designated S-4 that was located 15 miles south of Groom Lake, Nevada (Area 51). According to the articulate young 'physicist', whose name was later revealed to be Bob Lazar, the power source for this sleek, semi-lustrous saucer-shaped craft (which he dubbed "the Sport Model") was a basketball-sized anti-matter reactor that generated and focused gravity waves to distort space-time. Fuel for the reactor was the stable super-heavy element 115, a brittle, burnt-orange colored substance that doesn't occur naturally on earth. While in the "Omicron Configuration" the craft balanced on an out-of-phase gravity wave, but for interstellar flight, in order to warp or bend the fabric of space, gravity amplifiers were employed in what was known as the "Delta Configuration." When fully operational, these rendered part of the saucer invisible, thus explaining all the reported sightings of UFOs making abrupt turns and generally defying the laws of physics. Besides the so-called "Sport Model", Lazar said that he'd seen an assortment of nine different types of craft that were kept inside hangars disguised to look like the sides of the beige-and-brown hillocks. On one occasion, he might have even glimpsed a diminutive being that wasn't from this planet.

In what would seem to be a serious breach of his security oath, Lazar took several friends to the perimeter of the base on a pitch-black night that he knew the craft was scheduled to be test flown. From an unsurfaced road they watched with utter amazement as a strange luminous object performed erratic maneuvers in the restricted airspace above the Groom Mountains.

As the pulsating light continued to dart about, security patrols soon cornered them. Lazar tried to hide by running into the desert, but to no avail. After being detained and questioned for over an hour all were released. However, the following morning Lazar was subjected to verbal abuse while being interrogated by his superiors. For this indiscretion his security clearance was pulled and his work analyzing alien antigravity technology ended. Later, fearing for his safety, he decided to go public.

If stories involving the military being in possession of an alien craft caused a sensation, other claims by the bespectacled technician really strained credulity. For example, as part of the indoctrination process, along with briefing papers, Lazar said that he had been shown a strange book (which contained pictures similar to diffraction-grating 3-D images) that asserted that humans were a product of numerous genetic modifications, and were referred to merely as "containers" by the aliens. For our part, the extraterrestrial biological entities (EBEs) that originated in the binary Zeta Reticuli system were derisively called "the Kids." Even more startling, along with these evolutionary adjustments, was the artificial creation by the aliens of several spiritual leaders thousands of years in our past.

Needless to say, Lazar's startling revelations have made him a highly controversial figure in the world of ufology. Over the years his story has remained consistent, always recounted in a straightforward and emotionless tone. Showing refreshing restraint, he is careful not to speculate on matters that he personally didn't experience or that that he has limited knowledge of. To many this makes him more believable, or at least suggests that he truly believes what he claims to have witnessed. To some, however, he is an unwitting dupe, either as part of a controlled information leak, or to disseminate disinformation for some hidden agenda. What he was allowed to witness was staged for his behalf and intended to be circulated among the masses, though with a built-in 'poison pill' (such as the aliens' 'history' book) in the event that he needed to be discredited. Simply put, the 'alien hardware' story was allowed to be made public in order to protect what actually is being test flown at the base. Of course to others Lazar is a complete fraud – the entire S-4 story being nothing but a well-crafted hoax. Those who question his veracity point out that no one has yet been able to verify his education and employment records (although a W-2 form would seem to corroborate some of his claims). Believers counter that someone is attempting to make him disappear. He didn't learn what he knows by attending junior college. Besides, when questioned by a credible former Area 51 worker as to how he paid for his meals in the cafeteria there, Lazar had the correct answer.

While many were still undecided about Lazar's wild claims, out of the shadows came a new informant. This was a retired mechanical engineer who claimed that he worked on flight simulators at a secret compound to train human pilots how to operate the duplicated alien avionics. Going by the pseudonym of JAROD 2 – allegedly named after an extraterrestrial named JAROD who served as a technical advisor for the project – the elderly former program insider went on to describe many surprising technical details, but is more famously known in Area 51 lore for his claim that the aliens involved spoke "a higher form of Hungarian".

Though many laughed at this ludicrous notion, one researcher found some strategic plausibility in the assertion when he discovered that many leading scientists and engineers supposedly involved in the project were of Hungarian extraction. This included the physicist Edward Teller (E.T. himself). Being a very difficult tongue to understand, Hungarian (Magyar) would make for a rather secure system of communication in an already compartmentalized working environment, much in the same way that the nearly indecipherable Navajo language was chosen by the code talkers of WWII. In a parallel involving purported recovered alien technology, Hungarians are considered to be an isolated ethnic group (gypsies?) with a mysterious linguistic tradition, and a people who have long questioned their origins. At any rate, on a trip to Budapest, Area 51 aficionado Glenn Campbell found a phone book that contained many listings for the name Lazar – 422 to be precise. But again, is JAROD 2's story just another shiny diversion?

## Iconic Black Mailbox

At the height of the Lazar craze, UFO enthusiasts from all over the globe made the pilgrimage to a black mailbox situated on a large dirt pull out along Nevada Highway 375. Although just the ordinary mail drop of a local rancher, it also functioned as the roadside landmark for Area 51 sky-watchers. From this gathering place, believers and the curious alike trained optical devices under a brilliant canopy of stars, waiting for the ionized glow of a pewter-colored saucer to appear over the Groom Mountains. (The best viewing time was on Wednesday nights, coincidently "Spaghetti Night" at the "Little A-Le-Inn", a doublewide trailer-turned-bar and grill some 20 miles up the road.) If nothing dazzlingly conspicuous turned up, any bright illumination drew oohs and aahs from the faithful as video cameras captured whatever it was that shone through the light pollution of distant Las Vegas. Most often these were the lights of a 737, or from the "Janet flights" that commuted base workers. But to the UFO chasers it didn't matter; they saw what they wanted to see.

Not content with the motor home crowd watching from the Mailbox Road, a small group of black-budget aircraft buffs and anti-secrecy activists who called themselves the "Dreamland Interceptors"

The famous 'Black Mailbox' (photo by Blair MacKenzie Blake)

roamed the harsh desert terrain in camouflage fatigues – thus mocking the paramilitary security teams that patrolled the buffer zone. Rather than eat spaghetti at the A-Le-Inn, these patriotic gadflies dined on the more austere MREs (modern day K-rations) as they crept about the spiky yucca, wreaking havoc on the goons of a satellite government. When not dismantling magnetic trip sensors on BLM land, they marked their locations with signs upon which the word "SENSOR" was scrawled in fluorescent orange paint. And while sabotaging these high-tech security measures, they were always on the lookout for new high points from which to discern and photograph the aerodynamic schemes of the military's next generation aircraft. With their telephoto lenses, some might have even wondered what else might be parked in the garage?

## Space-Time Distortion on Campfire Hill

Plowing through sagebrush on khaki-colored dirt roads, dodging jack-rabbits and swarms of kangaroo mice, we arrived at our favorite camping spot near the border, knowing full well that the camou-dudes in ubiquitous white Jeep Cherokees were keeping a close watch on us. Along with the wail of coyotes, we could hear the faint whine of their generators while discreetly parked on a dirt spur. Once settled in our lawn chairs, we sipped beers and watched for anything unusual moving against the celestial tapestry. On previous trips we'd seen most of the explainable lights in the sky, including the Janet shuttle runs, strobing red dots (jets), and golden-orange orbs that were most likely infrared suppression flares employed during military exercises.

Despite the security personnel lurking about, the small hill on which we were seated was the perfect place to ponder Lazar's fantastic tale. Prior to feeling the lustrous sheen of the disc stored at S-4, Lazar had thought the whole notion of UFOs as being absolutely ridiculous. However, for a skeptic who didn't have any previous interest in the subject, as well as a limited knowledge of ufology's vast literature, there are certainly many similarities between his story and that of others. For example, his description of the "Sport Model" shares several unique features with the craft that logger

"Camou-dudes" keeping an eye on intruders from their patrol vehicles
(photo by by Chuck Clark)

Travis Walton claimed to have been inside after being abducted in 1975. Both describe the surfaces of the walls, floor and ceiling all curving perfectly into each other as if molded from a single quantity of material. Also, both commented on how the craft's metallic skin had the ability to become transparent under certain conditions. But what of Lazar's alien propulsion technology? There certainly would appear to be some flaws, especially when it comes to bending or folding space around the disc. In pulling the destination to the spacecraft, (or vice versa) wouldn't one greatly risk destroying it by colliding with everything in the path (no matter how narrow the course) of a focused gravity wave stretching for a hundred trillion miles? Or is cosmic geography and/or artificially created space objects somehow accounted for in the Delta Configuration?

I wasn't too concerned about Lazar's lack of credentials, the vagaries of gravity warp drives, or any clever pastiche. What bothered me was that nothing about his story seemed very alien. There are more imaginative accounts by witnesses who claimed that the interior of the spaceship they were in was considerably more spacious than it appeared from the outside, or that while observing the UFO from a distance, their eyesight suddenly had become greatly magnified with regards to clarity of detail. I would think that any recovered artifact that was truly otherworldly would be nauseatingly disorienting, so dissimilar would it be to our own creations. Whether the probe of space-faring colonists on an interstellar ark (artificial biosphere), or robotic scouts of a post-biological intelligence, or, for that matter, the lost new toy of a child whose species is immeasurably beyond the level of human intelligence, I could just imagine the pathetic bewilderment of Earth's greatest minds still trying some 60 years later to find the doorway into the damned thing, let alone understanding how it operates. Unless, that is, it was a dumbed down creation of advanced sentient beings and didn't in any way represent the pinnacle of their technological achievement.

This – something that humans could handle – they bequeathed to us (though possibly made to *appear* as if it crashed in order to be retrieved) so as to give us a nudge in the right direction…perhaps even to reshape our future.

Taking a gulp of beer, I had to remind myself never to make assumptions when it came to extraterrestrials. The spectrum of possibilities was endless. We shouldn't limit ourselves to the narrow perspective of any one academic discipline. Ultimately, the presence of alien visitors may be undetectable due to the limitations of human perception. Conversely, we might share a common genetic heritage with them, or they might come from a parallel-Earth whose technology is only slightly more advanced than ours. Of course if we turned out to be the conscious inhabitants of someone's simulated multiverse, then all bets would be off. As for Lazar having read that humans are considered to be "containers", this I liked. The Earth could very well be a preserve, with humans being someone's exclusive property. Containers for what, though, is anyone's guess. It could be something incomprehensible. Noting the indistinct shapes of cows grazing on the open range, it struck me that even if they had some inkling that they might end up as a "Double Whopper" on the menu at Burger King, could they ever conceive of one day being an autographed catcher's mitt on display in Cooperstown? Again, although I wasn't that impressed with Lazar's story, it was the only show in town. Besides, what if it was true? I certainly wanted to see "things that would make George Lucas drool."

Flying a secret aircraft painted black under the cover of darkness is one thing, but at Area 51, as it turned out, even the starry skies could be taken away. Case in point: while seated in my chair speculating about mysterious others in the infinitely inhabited cosmos, the next thing I remembered was having been awakened by my friend who was leaning inside the open tent flap holding open a plastic trash bag. "Are you going to be sick?" he asked. At that very moment I threw up, having a strange metallic taste in my mouth, sort of like charcoal lighter fluid. My friend told me that he had just woke up inside his tent and had puked. What the hell was going on? How'd I get inside my tent? Later it occurred to us that we had been gassed by someone and placed inside our tents. If indeed that was the case, was it to render us unconscious during some secret test flight, or just the camou-dudes having some fun? Even dastardlier, I think one of them tossed a scorpion into my sleeping bag.

## Aurora Roar on a Cheshire Airstrip?

Camping out on the hill another night, the desert silence was suddenly broken by a pulsed, deep-basso thrumming that was much louder than the ground-idling engines of jetfighters that we'd heard over the hills on previous occasions. This distinctive sound immediately brought to mind descriptions of the "sky-tearing" throbbing supposedly emitted by the mythical hypersonic spyplane known as the "Aurora". Powered by a liquid methane pulse-detonation wave engine, the delta-shaped craft is believed to be capable of reaching Mach 6 or higher.

In the early 1990s, a series of unexplained "skyquakes" that rattled windows and jarred nerves in southern California (always on Thursday mornings) fueled speculation that the Air Force was testing a new secret aircraft that represented a quantum leap in technology. Could these advances have something to do with the back-engineering of alien craft as described by JAROD-2? The former insider had made the distinction of stating that it was impossible for humans to pilot the alien discs, therefore they were being trained to operate the alien drive system when combined with our own technology. If the Aurora actually exists, it is most likely to be a space plane – an aircraft that can travel into outer space after taking off from a runway, as opposed to being lifted into orbit by a rocket like the Air Force's experimental unmanned X-37B orbital test vehicle. As for the runway itself, this might be Area 51's rumored "Cheshire Airstrip." According to several witnesses, this runway suddenly appears out of nowhere, only to quickly disappear again when not in use. Such a landing strip could be constructed to mimic the desert surroundings when not activated by special lighting, or could be a high-tech projection (hologram) on the playa. Though security forces didn't gas us that night, we never did see anything take to the air. We only heard the unforgettable sound.

## Exotic Aeroforms = Burnt Hotdogs

Over the years I've heard many sonic booms while UFO spotting near Dreamland. Normally these are from the various military aircraft such as B2 bombers and F-22 Raptors on routine maneuvers over the Tikaboo Valley. However, one night while grilling beef franks and watching the glittering skies for any disruption of stars – the tell-tale sign of "chameleons" utilizing camouflage receptors – a deafening report shook the desert floor. This was similar to both the sky-quakes that I felt in Los Angeles, and to the space shuttle re-entering Earth's atmosphere. Thinking it might have been from the Aurora returning to Groom Lake, I scanned the sky with a pair of binoculars. Once again I didn't see anything and was left to wonder what it might have been while poking at neglected burnt hotdogs.

That wouldn't be the only time that franks on the Weber became charred beyond recognition due to anomalous lights and sounds. While enjoying another space picnic, with the electronic music of Tomita for ambience, the secret base suddenly came to life. Dozens of ground-launched magnesium flares illuminated the runway over the hills as a Pave Hawk helicopter buzzed the nearby ridges. Next we could see a noisy C-130 Hercules flying in a wide circle. Through binoculars red darters appeared in each quadrant of the sky as if forming a protective barrier. Amid all this activity, someone

Pave Hawk helicopter buzzing the ridges surrounding Area 51
(photo by Blair MacKenzie Blake)

noticed a tiny green light very high in the sky. Barely perceptible at first, it descended with incredible speed, appearing as a cool white diamond-shaped object enhaloed with a spectral green plasma as it passed overhead and quickly disappeared behind a ridge where more brilliant golden-white flares hovered. Had we just witnessed the TR3-A Black Manta suborbital prototype? Or perhaps it was the tight-lipped Blackstar spacecraft? Whatever it was, I seriously doubt that we hit the Area 51 jackpot and saw a human-piloted alien craft.

## Media Circus on the E.T. Highway

With the dedication of the E.T. Highway in July 1996, I felt that I'd just about spent enough time driving down bone-jarring dirt and gravel roads, leaving in my wake plumes of plutonium-laden dust. I was growing tired of the intimidation tactics and psychological warfare games of the camou-dudes while seated along the perimeter of the vast military reserve, hoping to see something technologically shocking. Rumors still persisted about enormous silent black triangles (dirigibles?) as stealthy troop transports, and of nuclear-powered tactical reconnaissance craft whose propulsion system disrupted gravity. Even the "They're Here!" Lazar discs had been seen jumping about over the Groom Mountains.

Watching the celebration at the Little A-Le-Inn, I recalled having helped the owner put the two trailers together back before they even had an "Area 51 Visitor's Permit" bumper sticker for sale. Now there were alien-themed baubles galore as UFO enthusiasts, local ranchers, and anti-government conspiracy theorists talked about paradigm shifts, the Illuminati, and shape-shifting reptilians while eating "Alien Burgers" and drinking Milwaukee's Best. The colorful assemblage included some regular favorites, like the ambassador from a distant galaxy and a Japanese mortician who liked to sing country-western songs…when not warning people about anti-gravity saucers at Dreamland being pure theater designed to cause mass panic in order to enslave the populace and usher in the New World Order. There were also bits of conversation about boron-snatching EBEs who liked strawberry ice cream, the lunar landing hoax, and a government treaty with 'greys' allowing them to abduct humans and perform horrific genetic experiments in exchange for alien technology. By far the strangest of all though was a new bartender (Astro-American?) who appeared to be completely mystified by the concept of a simple bottle opener when one of us ordered a Heineken. As the famous Black Mailbox was being auctioned off, outside the "Interceptors" were involved in a political brouhaha. With all these vendors of kitschy glow-in-the-dark alien gimcracks, talk of milk carton kids, and rambling apocalyptic scenarios, there was only one thing left to do. Head for the nearby sun-baked hills, set up camp in the fragrance of burned sagebrush, and wait for the stars to come out one by one…

The Little A-Le-Inn (photo by Blair MacKenzie Blake)

## Multirole Aerial Drone in a Margarita

Although it was a moonless night, there hadn't been any activity over the base as I handed my friend a margarita that I had prepared in a large plastic cup. After taking a sip, he spat it out, thinking that a bug, perhaps a large moth, was floating inside it. After a second sip, he again quickly expelled the contents from his mouth. Checking the cup with a flashlight, he was horrified to see a strange insect whose length was almost the same diameter as the cup. Instinctively, he tossed the thing, along with the margarita, out into the desert. Before doing so, however, I had gotten a glimpse of it, and to me, while resembling a dragonfly, it appeared somewhat artificial looking with its whitish, matte-grey color. So strange was it, that I spent nearly an hour searching the area with my own flashlight.

Unable to find it in the morning as well, today I can't help but think that it was an insect-sized spy drone. The Air Force has admitted to having a microaviary of drones designed to replicate the flight mechanics of birds, so why not dragonflies as well?

## TR3 or Tier III?

Could the reality behind all the 'noise' of alien craft at Area 51 be the testing of Unmanned Aerial Vehicles (UAVs) piloted by "Captain NOLO" (No Live Operator), along with the militarization of space by 'futuristic' craft like the Aurora, supposedly equipped with particle beam weapons to protect our orbiting satellites? Drones had become an Area 51 priority decades ago, beginning with the stealthy black D-21 that was launched from a B-52. Looking at it in this light, could the rumored TR3-A be a misnomer – a phonetic corruption of TIER III, itself the designation of a certain class of satellite telemetry drones such as the RQ-3 DarkStar? If so, one certainly hopes that remotely piloted vehicles with optically transparent skins, or chameleons that take on their surroundings – drones with ominous sounding names like "Predator", "Reaper", "Sentinel" and "Global Hawk" – aren't misused as part of an expanding surveillance state (i.e. in the backyards of fellow citizens). Ironically, in making all those trips to the perimeter of the secret base – hoping to catch a glimpse of something that was allegedly conceived on another world – my friends and I (along with many others attracted to the area) might have served the military's purpose quite well by providing them with unsuspecting 'targets' for the various UAVs being tested there. High tech drones certainly could explain many of the sightings of strange alien shapes performing irregular maneuvers as witnessed by saucer chasers, even though "Captain NOLO" doesn't like strawberry ice cream.

**Blair MacKenzie Blake** has been studying, practicing, and writing about the western esoteric tradition for over twenty years. He is the author of two books: *Ijynx* and *The Wickedest Books in the World: Confessions of an Aleister Crowley Bibliophile*. In his 'other life', he is the writer/content manager for www.toolband.com and www.dannycarey.com.

# THE Uninvited

## WHEN THE SPIRITS RETURNED TO ICELAND, THEY DIDN'T COME TO PLAY

by *Greg Taylor*

In the shadow of Christmas 1908, almost one hundred people sat quietly within a heated hall as another long Icelandic winter's night began. The sound of scuffing feet and low murmurs dominated the hall, as the tense crowd waited for a glimpse of the young man they had come to see. When he finally emerged from an adjoining room, the handsome 25-year-old strolled with purpose towards the pulpit at the centre of one end of the room. Seating himself at the nearby table – the only one in the room – he nodded to the official already seated and waiting for him. The white noise of the room died a sudden death; another official surveyed the crowd silently, instructed one man to lock the doors to the hall, and then another to put out the lamp illuminating the room.

Suddenly another light source appeared: a candle, lit beside the harmonium player, who launched into a hymn medley, accompanied by several people in the audience. The young man sat motionless on his chair for a long while, his hands clasped at his chest, as if in prayer. Then, suddenly his head and hands fell, as if a puppeteer had loosed his strings. The lead official signaled to the harmonium player, who brought the hymnal accompaniment to a close as the candle was extinguished. As the light died, the assembled group caught one last glimpse of the young man, as the official seated beside him suddenly grabbed his arms forcefully. The whole hall seemed to suck inward through pure weight of the tension in the air, as darkness enveloped all and through the silence only deep breathing could be heard.

And then, a voice sliced through the stillness, simultaneously making one hundred hearts jump. From the general area of the pulpit, with little fanfare, the dead had made their appearance. Talking through the entranced medium, the 'control' personality greeted all those present and introduced himself. Then, behind the crowd, another of the dead announced itself, and again, to the side of the hall a woman's voice addressed the audience in French. From the front of the hall the official called confirmation, "I am still holding his arms!".

A strong breeze rushed across the hall, confusing those who knew the doors and windows of the hall were locked shut. Cracking sounds were heard in the air, bringing the tension to fever pitch, when the harmonium player began shouting. He had felt the instrument begin lifting off the floor, and had thrust his left foot onto the floor while keeping his right foot on one of the pedals, in order to steady himself. Nevertheless, as the harmonium continued to bob across the floor he was compelled to jump along with it, until it was suddenly snatched away. The official immediately called for the lights to be turned back on, and those present were stunned to find the harmonium had been moved on top of a table on the east side of the hall, though nobody had heard any sound of it moving there or being put onto the table.

It took two men to lift the roaming instrument down from its perch, and they did so with some difficulty – and not without some noise.

The young man at the centre of this maelstrom woke from his trance, blinking at the bright lights. Not yet fully awake, he staggered from the hall, barely able to remain upright, apparently unaware of the extraordinary happenings in the hall just minutes before.

## Birth of a Medium

Indridi Indridason was born October 12$^{th}$, 1883, and grew up as the uneducated son of a farmer in a rural area in the western part of Iceland. In 1905 he travelled to the Icelandic capital of Reykjavik to take up a job as a printer's apprentice with the weekly newspaper *Isafold*. The young man's life may have continued in obscurity if it wasn't for a chance invitation from a relative, with whom he was staying, to attend a rather odd type of meeting.

The turn of the century was the golden age of Spiritualism. The previous few decades had seen the birth of the prestigious Society for Psychical Research (SPR), and genuine scientific investigation into 'superstar' mediums such as D.D. Home, Leonora Piper and Eusapia Palladino. Publications by members of the SPR were read widely by academics, and in 1903 the prominent Icelandic writer Einar Hjörleifsson Kvaran wrote a positive story on the evidence for life after death, inspired by the post-humous release of Frederic Myers' seminal book *Human Personality and Its Survival of Bodily Death*.

Kvaran didn't limit his interest to just theory though; he decided to 'get his hands dirty' as well by taking the lead of the SPR and forming his own experimental circle, despite there being no reports at all of Icelandic mediums up till that point. As such, Kvaran and his group of friends forged ahead with some self-experimentation, beginning with attempts at automatic writing and 'table-tilting'. Kvaran would later relate how he came to discover the talents of

Indridi Indridason

Indridason accidentally in 1905, when the young man attended one of these table-tilting meetings with his relative Indridi Einarsson and his wife, with whom he was staying after recently moving to the Icelandic capital:

> Indridi Einarsson was interested in the experiments but his wife much more so. Once when she sat by a table Indridi came along. She asked him to participate in that experiment.
>
> Indridi had hardly taken his seat, when the table reacted violently and trembled. Indridi became frightened and was going to run out of the house.
>
> From that time the experiments with Indridi started.
>
> He came to my home and we sat down at a table. The table trembled, shook, and moved violently around in the room and nearly broke. Once it was overturned.

Kvaran questioned Indridason as to whether he had ever experienced strange things before this point, who replied that he had previously had some "remarkable visions". As for the possibility that he was a budding performance magician, the young man claimed to have never heard of mediumistic phenomena, nor have seen performers such as conjurors and jugglers, due to his upbringing in the rural west of the country.

With Indridason's ability at table-tilting obvious, Kvaran and his experimental circle began testing their star subject with automatic writing, an alleged method of receiving messages from the great beyond where the medium empties their mind and begins writing without conscious control. Indridason apparently succeeded immediately, with the messages from the dead offering a number of "proofs of identity", according to Kvaran.

Then, on the weekend before Easter 1905, while attempting more automatic writing at Kvaran's home, Indridason fell into trance for the first time. The young medium had been making irreverent jokes at the expense of the 'personality' that he believed was sending messages through him, which seemed to upset the otherworldly ghostwriter. Indridason's hand all of a sudden wrote "You should not make fun of me", followed quickly by the message "Indridi shall now fall into trance". The control instructed Indridason to put his head down on a pillow on a table, and the others present to turn out the light; he lost consciousness a few minutes later and began to write. According to Kvaran, Indridason…

> …wrote a few sentences with harsh jerks, and sighed heavily and screamed from time to time. He spoke with someone he obviously thought of as being with him, asked him not to treat him badly and expressed disagreement with what he thought was being said to him. Then, after about an hour, he was woken up, apparently by the same force that had put him to sleep. He was woken at our request; as we had never seen this stage before and we were uneasy.

Kvaran was persuaded by these early phenomena to step up the investigation into Indridason. His experimental circle was formalized as 'The Experimental Society' in the autumn of 1905, with the express intention of studying Indridi Indridason's strange talents. Its founding members included the highest members of Icelandic society, from Kvaran himself to Bjorn Jonsson, who would later become Prime Minister of Iceland. This research group became the sole agent for Indridason's mediumship, paying him a modest yearly salary on the proviso that he take part in no other séances without direct permission from the Society. They also built a small house for him, giving him free lodging, but for the main purpose of being better able to study him in an environment they felt they had control over. The Experimental Society held sittings with Indridason once or twice a week throughout the year, only taking a short two-month break during the summer months.

## Manifestation Destiny

In late 1905, the table tilting became table levitations. While Indridason was visiting with friends on a November evening in Reykjavik, the table they were sitting around rose up suddenly and bumped into their faces. Three of the men present attempted to push the table down, but failed to get it back to the floor, despite Indridason sitting with his hands above the table. In another séance shortly after, "peculiar" cracking sounds were heard in the air, moving all around the room, while the young medium remained completely still in his seat. And then the lights began to appear...

In their first appearance, sitters saw the lights floating through the air and on the walls of the room, sometimes flashing. Over successive séances, the phenomena seemed to grow more robust and diverse. Kvaran wrote of this phenomenon that the lights...

> ...had somewhat different color, some very white, others were more reddish. Once, during an experimental séance at my home, 58 lights were counted. These lights were of various shapes: some of the lights were round while others were oblong. They were of different sizes: some were small, about an inch in diameter, but others were stripes of light around two to four feet long...

> There were a few times when light spread behind the medium on a whole wall, which was twelve feet wide and ten feet high. Sometimes it looked like a sort of net of light, with circular meshes: slightly darker circles around bright flashes. Again the light was

sometimes continuous, similar to the glow from a great fire. Those spreads of light were never as white as the small lights were, but were more reddish.

Before each appearance of the lights, the sitters usually felt gusts of wind in the séance room, strong enough to mess up their hair and flap the pages of the researcher's notebooks. The peculiar clicking and cracking sounds previously observed often accompanied the light show as well, while Indridason himself seemed to go through a painful ordeal during their manifestation. Kvaran noted that immediately preceding the appearance of the lights, Indridi would begin to shriek and scream, and would continue doing so while they remained. After séances, the medium would say that he "felt as if he had been beaten up."

And then, the dead appeared in person. In a sitting on December 6, 1905, soon after the lights had made their appearance, sitters were shocked to find they were not alone in the room. In the reddish glow of the anomalous luminescence, the torso and head of a man was seen, standing with his back to the group, some eight to ten feet from where the medium was sitting, still shrieking in pain. Students of the paranormal might recognize some similarities here with other cases, such as the investigation of poltergeist phenomena surrounding Doris Bither in the 1970s, in which researchers claimed to have seen the materialization of the upper body of a man during a manifestation of anomalous light phenomena.

On other occasions, sitters reported seeing a "luminous, beautiful light-pillar" appear, slightly larger than a human being, inside of which they could make out the form of a human figure. The appearance of the light-pillar was accompanied by a low buzzing sound (an interesting facet, for those who have read my previous essay on paranormal sounds), and soon after it would resolve into a fully-fledged, luminous human body:

Einar Hjorleifsson Kvaran

The medium was in a very deep trance. The new visitor was dressed in very fine white drapery, of which many folds hung down to the floor; and the light was radiating from him. We saw him at different places in the room. Once he stood on a sofa, and behind him was a red light, which was similar to a little sun, with whitish light streaming out from it. This sight I shall never forget. Frequently he managed to appear 7-8 times the same evening in different places in the room. Many times we saw the medium and this materialized being simultaneously. But this extraordinary visitor could not be visible for more than a few seconds each time. When he had finished showing himself he tried to touch a few sitters with his hand, arm or foot, and he always allowed us to touch his materialized body before he dematerialized it again.

On multiple occasions, witnesses noted that during these manifestations Indridason was visible in the ghostly luminosity thrown by the apparition. The figure in the room was not him.

## A Dark and Frightening Change

Sittings with Indridason continued to yield strange phenomena. On a number of occasions, his left arm was said to be 'dematerialized' by his controls, with those present unable to find it via touch or in the glow of lit matches. The medium also began to be levitated himself, with sitters reporting that they could hear him being dragged along the ceiling, some 12 feet high. And there were also instances of apports – objects appearing in the séance room, seemingly out of thin air – and manifestations of strong, fragrant odors, a staple of physical mediumship and other Fortean phenomena.

One of the more evidential events at this time was an apparent case of 'traveling clairvoyance', very similar to the famed story regarding the Swedish mystic Emanuel Swedenborg. A discarnate personality, introducing himself as "Mr. Jensen", said he had just been in the Danish capital of Copenhagen, where he had witnessed firemen overcoming a factory fire. The researchers immediately realized the possibility of this being investigated further – at that time there was no instantaneous communication link between Iceland and Denmark. They noted the time of Mr. Jensen's statement, and the next day went to the Bishop of Iceland in order for him to witness the claim. A month later, when the next boat arrived from Denmark, a scan of the newspapers revealed that there had indeed been a factory fire at this time.

But in September 1907, one event seems to have precipitated a dark and frightening change in the mediumship of Indridi Indridason. While visiting a village on an island off the southern coast of Iceland, he reported seeing the apparition of a man, one Jon Einarsson, who had drowned himself a year earlier. Upon returning to Reykjavik, strange disturbances started occurring in the rooms which Indridason shared with theology student Thordur Oddgeirsson, and at subsequent séances. The medium also reported that he was having continued visions of the same man he had seen on the island.

Then, during a séance on December $7^{th}$, the controls reported to the group that "Jon" was now in attendance, and was in control of "the power", and in a very bad mood. Indridason went into convulsions, sitters felt their clothing and hats being grabbed at, and a full coal-scuttle was thrown, barely missing one of the sitters. Later that night, when Indridason and Oddgeirsson went to bed, a plate flew from the front room into the bedroom, and the medium's bed was pulled suddenly out from the wall. Indridason was reportedly terrified by this development – regular sittings were canceled for some time, and members of the Experimental Society had to stay with him at night to calm his nerves.

The following night, Kvaran stayed to reassure the terror-stricken medium, locking the doors to the building and staying in the bedroom with him and the theology student after the lights were put out. Suddenly, Indridason fell into a trance, and his chief control told Kvaran that "Jon" had just gone to get power, and this was very serious. The medium woke from his trance, but then things began to happen:

> [T]he ends of the bed in which the medium and Mr. Oddgeirsson were lying were raised and lowered alternately and the bed shaken. The medium was lying on the side farther from the wall. He shouted that he was being dragged out of the bed, and was very terror-stricken. He implored Mr. Oddgeirsson to hold onto his hand. Mr. Oddgeirsson took his hand, pulling with all his might, but could not hold him. The medium was lifted above the end of the bed against which his head had been lying, and was pulled down onto the floor, sustaining some injuries to his back from the bedstead. At the same moment a pair of boots, which had been under Mr. Oddgeirsson's bed, were thrown at the lamp, breaking both the glass and the shade.

Indridason was then dragged headfirst out the door of the bedroom and into the front room, despite desperately trying to grab hold of pieces of furniture, and having both Kvaran and Oddgeirsson pulling at his legs. They finally managed to get him back to his bed with great difficulty, but his legs were then lifted so forcefully that the two men could not push them back down to the bed.

Their reaction to these events was a natural one: they got out of the house as fast as possible, went to Kvaran's home, and turned on all the lights! Nevertheless, phenomena continued – a book flew off a table and hit a hanging lamp in the drawing room, then continued on and hit another smaller lamp; a pot plant shifted a few inches; and knocks were heard on the walls of the room.

The poltergeist phenomena continued on subsequent nights, to varying degrees. On December 10$^{th}$, the Experimental Society's harmonium player (and also organist at Reykjavik Cathedral)

Brynjolfur Thorlaksson stayed with Indridason and Oddgeirsson, sleeping on a couch in the front room. Indridason once again fell into a trance, and the controls warned that "Jon" had gathered "considerable" power during the day. Two candlesticks were flung to the floor, and a brush was thrown across the room. Indridason then began screaming that "Jon" was there. Thorlaksson went to the bedroom and lay on top of Indridason, and had to use all his strength to hold him down. Oddgeirsson went to his aid, but a bedside table was smashed over his shoulders – he jumped back into his bed and pulled the quilt over his head, but the table continued to bash him mercilessly.

The accosted trio managed to light a lamp and began planning their escape from the building. Indridason started to get dressed, and was putting on his trousers when he was flung down onto the bed again. Thorlaksson rushed to help when a bowl flew from a chest of drawers in the bedroom straight for him. He dodged the missile, but reported that after it passed him the bowl changed direction and smashed into a stove in the outer room. Continuing on into the bedroom to assist the frightened medium, Thorlaksson was gobsmacked by what he witnessed:

> [A] vision that I shall never forget. Indridi is lying horizontal in the air, at about the height of my chest, and swaying there to and fro, with his feet pointing towards the window, and it seems to me that the invisible power that is holding him in the air is trying to swing him out of the window. I don't hesitate a moment, but grab around the medium where he is swinging in the air, and push him down onto the bed and hold him there. But then I notice that both of us are being lifted up. I scream to Thordur Oddgeirsson and ask him to come help.

Upon hearing the call for help, the theology student made for the bedroom, only to have a chair hurled at him by some invisible force. Side-stepping the hostile furniture, he continued to the bedroom where he saw Thorlaksson lying on the chest of the medium, whose whole body was in motion. He spread his weight across Indridason's knees to assist, when the two candlesticks from the front room drifted into the room and were flung onto the floor beside them.

The three men linked arms and began backing out of the room, with Oddgeirsson holding the lamp before them to illuminate any further threats. A hand-basin flew towards them from a table in the bedroom at head-height, then changed direction and smashed into the stove in the outer room, breaking to pieces. At 2.30 a.m., three grown men rushed out of the house into the Icelandic night, terrified.

If the physical violence wasn't intimation enough that this new presence was a dangerous one, the threat soon became explicit. On December 17th, while staying at Kvaran's house, Indridason once again fell into trance. But this time something was different. Through choking sounds, it became clear that the usual controls were not in charge of the medium's body – instead, "Jon" began mumbling and swearing at those present. He then described Indridason as "a trained instrument which he should like to use at his pleasure", expressing his desire "to kill him and to do all possible harm to those in the so-called upper world". This seems to have spurred the other controls to combine forces and expel "Jon" from the medium's body, and diminish his influence. Curiously, as the malevolent spirit was being exorcised, sitters described hearing a buzzing sound surrounding Indridason. But the effort seems to have been a successful one, as Jon's power seemed to weaken from this point – so much so that he eventually appears to have reconciled and made peace with the medium and the experimental group.

## The Investigator Versus the Uninvited

Given the high profile of members of the Experimental Society, not least within the world of publishing and newspapers, the extraordinary tales surrounding the Indridason investigation were soon headline news in Iceland. He became one of the most well-known identities in the country, and – just as in the modern day – this led to plenty of accusations of deception, and calls for independent scientific investigation. On the back of the widespread publicity, one of the most respected scientists in Iceland, Dr. Gudmundur Hannesson – who in his life would serve as President of the University of Iceland, found the Icelandic Scientific Society, and spend 35 years as the Professor of Medicine at the University – requested permission to study Indridason. Noted for his integrity, though openly skeptical about the Experimental Society's reports regarding Indridason, Hannesson appeared to be the perfect candidate for external investigation of the phenomena. As such, the Experimental Society agreed to allow the respected professor to study Indridason.

Hannesson examined the Experimental House closely for any sort of hidden compartments or trapdoors that could conceal an accomplice or tools that would allow Indridason to fake the phenomena, but found none. When Indridason arrived for the séance, he would have to undress in bright light before Hannesson, and was given simple attire by the skeptical investigator to wear for the duration of the test. Hannesson then checked his hair for any tools of trickery.

The hall where the séance was held also had a makeover, with Hannesson installing a floor to ceiling net that divided the room into two parts, made of mesh "so small that it is quite impossible to get a hand through them". The medium and the watchman would be isolated on one side of the net, with the experimenters observing – as best as possible – from the other side of the net, guarding the single slit that provided access. Before beginning the séance, Hannesson made absolutely sure that there were no avenues for hoaxing by the medium:

> No effort is now spared in examining everything as minutely as possible. The hall is searched from floor to ceiling, and also every article that is in it. Nothing seems too trivial to be suspected that it may in some way serve the purpose of the impostors.

Gudmundur Hannesson

> This is no joke, either. It is a life-and-death struggle for sound reason and one's own conviction against the most execrable form of superstition and idiocy. No, certainly nothing must be allowed to escape.

And yet, once the doors were locked, and the lights turned off, extraordinary phenomena began almost immediately. Appearing shortly after Indridason went into trance, his controls noted that this séance might be unusually noisy, as some new and uninvited "visitors" had manifested. Voices were then heard in different parts of the hall, mumbling and cursing, before objects began to be thrown about the room with great force. Hannesson and his offsider instantly lit a match, but only saw Indridason and the watchman holding his hands, sitting in the same position as the watchman had reported during the commotion.

Then, the "spirits" turned things up a notch. The chairs beneath the medium and the watchman were snatched away and thrown into a corner of the room. The watchman, determined to continue holding onto Indridason, asked Hannesson to fetch the chairs for him. Lighting a match, the perplexed investigator noted the two men still in the centre of the room, only now standing, and one of the chairs lying in the corner of the room.

> I make for it, and in spite of the dark I find it at once. The very moment that I turn round to take the chair *I am struck a heavy blow in the back* [Hanneson's emphasis], as it were with a closed fist. Yet a few seconds previously there was nothing to be seen in that corner. I forthwith take the chair to the men and find them standing exactly as before.

Hannesson returned the chairs and retired to his observing station outside the net. A few moments later, the watchman shouted with urgency that things were "getting serious" – Indridason had been drawn up into the air with his feet towards the ceiling and his head toward the floor. The watchman exclaimed that he was trying to pull him back towards the floor, but that the force levitating Indridason had him at the limit of his strength to keep hold of the entranced medium. Then, all of a sudden, the pull slackened, and the medium sank back down slowly and the watchman put him back in his chair.

The reason for this (momentary) respite became clear when the voices of the "uninvited visitors" spoke in the dark, noting that they were going away for a short time to "get more power". Upon their return, the chairs beneath the medium and watchman were repeatedly snatched from beneath them, and eventually broken into pieces. Then…

> …the medium is pulled up into the air with so much force that the watchman, as he says, is repeatedly almost lifted off the ground. All this is accompanied by so much scuffling and struggling that apparently it is going to be unavoidable to go to the aid of the watchman, who is exerting himself not to let the medium go – up into the air!
>
> The scuffle is now carried towards the lectern. Suddenly the watchman shouts that things have taken a dangerous turn, for the medium's legs have been quickly pulled down into the lectern while the small of his back is resting on the edge. He fears that the medium will not be able to stand this and that it will result in disaster, for while he is pulling at his shoulders with all his strength "the others" are pulling at his legs.
>
> We are about to go inside to give assistance, when we hear some still rougher shuffling and the watchman says that everything is again all right. He has, he explains, put one foot against the lectern and in that way been able to pull the medium out and get him on the floor. The tumult now ceases.

Once again the "uninvited visitors" spoke up, cursing and threatening Indridason, and then once again retreating momentarily in order to "fetch more power." Again, there was no mistaking their return. With a terrific crash, the lectern was completely ripped from the wall and flung across the hall, and both the watchman and the medium were thrown into the air. The Reverend Haraldur Nielsson, who was acting as the watchman during this séance, described the turn of events:

> After a terrible struggle with two vulgar entities, while I kept my arms round the shoulders of the medium, pressing his legs between my knees, a pulpit situated near the wall inside the net and solidly fastened by nails to the floor had its panels all of a sudden jerked upwards from the floor and flung outwards to the net. It will be observed that this involved wrenching the woodwork out of the floor as well as from the wall, the pulpit being firmly fixed to both. After this I myself while continuing to hold the medium was thrown with him up into the air, so that we crashed to the floor violently, I with the result of swollen hands, he with a little perceptible sore caused by a nail upon which he fell.

The lectern was thrown with such force that it was now lying against the dividing net. Hannesson, on the other side from Indridason and Nielsson, grabbed hold of the corner, and called out to the undead vandals, challenging them to pull it from his grasp. A menacing voice growled out of the darkness, "Eat hell!", and the lectern was pulled away from Hannesson with significant force. The plucky investigator, for his part, replied to his ghostly antagonist with his own "uncomplimentary term", and was answered in turn with a face-full of broken glass and other debris. According to Hannesson, this was "thrown from the empty quarter and from a *different direction* [Hannesson's emphasis] entirely to that of the medium and the watchman, who were lying on the floor close to my feet." Hannesson was at a loss to explain what had just taken place: "Who in the world was it that threw these things?", he exclaimed.

Turning the lights on, the investigators surveyed the destruction: smashed chairs, the lectern in pieces, and an empty, unpainted space in the room where the lectern had once stood.

Hannesson continued to investigate the mediumship of Indridi Indridason for the whole winter, constantly trying to detect fraud. But he was never able to ascertain any trickery; "on the contrary, the bulk of the phenomena were, as far as I could judge, quite genuine, whatever their cause may have been."

Many years later, when Reverend Neilsson was leaving to attend a conference in Copenhagen on psychical research, Hannesson told him: "You may state as my firm conviction, that the phenomena are unquestionable realities."

## Those That Burn Brightest...

Indridason's mediumship was put under the microscope almost constantly until 1909, when, on a trip to visit his parents in the summer of 1909, both he and his fiancée contracted typhoid fever. Indridason survived, barely; his betrothed did not. The illness brought his mediumship to an end, after just four short years of producing some of the most remarkable phenomena ever witnessed in a séance room. Indridason would go on to marry another girl, with whom he had a daughter. But it seemed almost as if death had become his true companion: the baby died before reaching two years of age, and soon after Indridason himself contracted tuberculosis, resulting in his own death on 31$^{st}$ August, 1912. He was just 29.

The case of Indridi Indridason seems to embody the old saying, 'those who burn brightest, burn fastest'. In just four years, and aged only in his 20s, he produced *all* of the classic phenomena associated with physical mediumship: raps, lights, levitation (of both objects and himself), apports, self-playing musical instruments, voices, anomalous odors, breezes in closed rooms, and even supposed materializations of human figures. This despite there being no real tradition or knowledge of Spiritualism, nor conjuring tricks, in Iceland at the time of his discovery – a factor that only seems to be enhanced as a consequence of his rural upbringing.

So what are we to make of this case, a century on from Indridason's passing? For me, personally, the requirement by the 'spirit controls' of total darkness during the séances is an almost insurmountable problem – it positively screams fraud. Members of the Experimental Society even tried dim red light, thinking it might not have such an impact, but it still caused the phenomena to diminish. However, we can't just discard the case by assuming that Indridason was a talented hoaxer who did magic tricks in the dark. We also have to contend with the numerous instances of 'poltergeist' phenomena that occurred in full light, apparently spontaneously, which were viewed by multiple witnesses. Added to that are instances where investigators turned on lights at short notice without noticing anything untoward. For example:

> Hannesson once unintentionally switched on an electric torch without asking for permission. He heard one of the "ghosts" shout, close under his nose: "You damned scoundrel!". At the same time the torch flashed and lit up the whole inner area. Hannesson saw Indridason hanging limp in his chair in the same position as the watchman had stated, and everybody sitting still in their own seats.

The other possibility that comes to mind is that Indridason had an accomplice (or accomplices), allowing him to stay seated and guarded, while they worked their 'magic'. This would help explain objects moving to different parts of the hall, and incidents where multiple 'spirit voices' – including a woman who spoke in French – talked or sang simultaneously. For instance, Neilsson noted:

I have often heard two voices speaking or singing loudly, while I was sitting alone with the medium inside the net...holding both his hands and talking with the control.

Sometimes the control spoke through the medium while the voices were singing, but more often he was silent while the singing was going on but started speaking the moment it ceased.

Hannesson was especially wary of this possibility, as he felt the medium was too well-guarded, and unable to return to his seat with enough speed and silence. "I was on the whole more suspicious of such an assistant than of the medium himself," he once commented. But how did such an accomplice make his way into the isolated area that Hannesson had set up, given the net and the investigators' careful scan of the space for hidden spaces and trapdoors? And how did they make a getaway in those cases where a light was turned on at short notice, leaving no time for an intruder to disappear? To Hannesson, this factor alone "precluded that a man who might have been in the inner quarter could escape."

Nevertheless, various elements of the case continually provoke the skeptical mind. Indridason was apparently a rural lad who could barely write, let alone speak in other languages – but his grandfather's brother Konrad Gislason (who became his third 'spirit control') had been a professor of Icelandic at the University of Copenhagen in Denmark. On one occasion, sitters were amazed with Indridason performing some "remarkable" gymnastic feats while in the trance state, "which were so complex and difficult that Olafur Rosinkrans, who was a gymnastics education instructor, could not repeat them". Society members put this down to some sort of paranormal influence, but is it suggestive that – like many conjurors and escape artists – Indridason used his fitness and gymnastic ability to create 'magic' in the séance room, such as the 'levitations' where his feet were drawn up toward the ceiling? Perhaps the most concerning of all is the time when – on a rare occasion when a flash photographer had been allowed into the séance room – Indridason seems to have been caught using bedsheets to try and create a ghostly effect.

It is, all in all, enough for me – as someone who demands an extremely high threshold of evidence – to file the case under "probable fraud". Nevertheless, there is no shortage of incidents that seem to defy rational explanation, assuming the original reports are accurate, so I am unwilling to discard it completely. To give one quick example: on one occasion the Experimental Society decided to ask for an apport from the spirits, to be fetched from someone's house – the identity of whom they decided *after* the medium had gone into trance. Not only did the spirits bring them an item from this house, almost instantaneously, but they also described the scene at the visited house (three men sitting near the item, talking) accurately.

But even in the case of fraud, questions arise. Perhaps the most significant of which is: why would Indridason assemble such a formidable conjuring skill-set, only to be 'accidentally' discovered and undertake four whole years of testing for only a modest yearly payment, when he probably could have made a lot more (and been in a lot less danger of discovery) by setting out on his own as either a performing magician or a fake medium? Perhaps this was a long-term goal, cut short by his illness and death, but it seems unlikely. And given that many of the séance phenomena appear to have required an accomplice, who was it, and why were they partnered with Indridason?

Hannesson himself struggled with reconciling his natural skepticism with what he observed during his experiments:

> After prolonged observation I saw no way round the inference that the things move often, if not always, in an altogether unaccountable manner, without anybody's either directly or indirectly causing their movements by ordinary means. But although I cannot get away from this conclusion, I am utterly unable to bring myself to believe in it

altogether. It is not easy for unbelieving people to accept the theory that inanimate things move about without any natural causes.

If nothing else, the case of Indridi Indridason makes for a terrific, creepy, Fortean tale. A medium tested by top scientists and academics for almost four years, convincing them all that something paranormal was going on. Séances with hostile and physically aggressive spirits that could have come straight out of a 1980s horror movie. A fantastically talented young man – either as a medium, or a trickster – whose own life was a tragedy. And all occurring at the turn of the century, the age of the great mediums, a period that seems to be almost immersed in a paranormal fog.

And as a parting note, I can't but help provoke the interested Fortean into one last bit of fun contemplation as to whether there could be any possible link between Indridi Indridason, of Iceland, and the strange, otherworldly man who turned up in West Virginia during the birth of another Fortean mystery, the Mothman – an individual who called himself 'Indrid Cold'…

**Greg Taylor** is the owner and editor of the online alternative news portal, *The Daily Grail* (www.dailygrail.com), and is also the editor of *Darklore*. He is widely read in topics that challenge the orthodox worldview, from alternative history to the mysteries of human consciousness. Greg currently resides in Brisbane, Australia. He is currently working on a book surveying the evidence for an afterlife.

Due to many of the original reports on Indridi Indridason's mediumship being published in Icelandic, this essay is based largely on (and fully acknowledges its debt to) two sources: "The Icelandic Physical Medium Indridi Indridason", by Loftur R. Gissurarson and Erlendur Haraldsson (*Proceedings of the Society for Psychical Research* Vol. 57, Part 214, January 1989), and *Icelandic Spiritualism*, by Loftur Reimar Gissurarson and William H. Swatos, Jr.

# THE EXECUTABLE DREAMTIME

**"MAGIC IS THE CHEAT CODES FOR THE WORLD, SENDING A SIGNAL TO REALITY'S OPERATING SYSTEM."**
**— PLANETARY #7**

by *Mark Pesce*

Being Imbolc, the Illumination of all things Hidden and Occult, the holiday of Bride, who brings the Light of Knowledge to all those who humbly ask Her Grace to dispel Darkness, it is Meet and Proper to discuss Such Things as may lead to a Broader Understanding of the Relation between Word and Will. Once Requested, Thrice Granted. So mote it be!

## Word and Will

*I pitied thee,*
*Took pains to make thee speak, taught thee each hour*
*One thing or other: when thou didst not, savage,*
*Know thine own meaning, but wouldst gabble like*
*A thing most brutish, I endow'd thy purposes*
*With word that made them known.*

– *The Tempest*, Act I, Scene 2

A recent issue of *New Scientist* celebrated William S. Burroughs' most famous maxim: "Language is a virus." It seems that language, our ability to apprehend and manipulate symbols and signs, has evolved to fill a unique ecological niche – the space between our ears. Human beings, together with most higher animals, share an ability to sequence perceptual phenomena temporally, detecting the difference between before, during, and after. This capability is particularly pronounced in the primates, and, in the case of *Homo sapiens*, left us uniquely susceptible to an infection of sorts, an appropriation of our innate cognitive abilities for ends beyond those determined by nature alone. Our linguistic abilities aren't innate. They are not encoded in our DNA. Language is more like *E. coli*, the bacteria in our gut, symbiotically helping us to digest our food. Language helps us to digest phenomena, allowing us to ruminate on the nature of the world.

Why language at all? We are fairly certain that it confers evolutionary advantage, that a species which speaks (and occasionally, listens) is more likely to pass its genes on than a species which cannot speak. But we can't make too much of that: nearly all other animals are dumb, to varying degrees, and they manage to be fruitful and multiply without having to talk about it. Despite the fact that gorillas can sign and dolphins squeak, we haven't found any indication of the symbol-rich internal consciousness which we attribute to language. This means that other animals have a direct experience of the world around them, while everything we do is utterly infused with the fog of language.

We need to be clear about this: from the time, some tens or hundreds of years ago, that language invaded and colonized our cerebrums, we have increasingly lost touch with the reality of things. Reality has been replaced with relation, a mapping of *things-as-they-are* to *things-as-we-believe-them-to-be*. Language allows us to construct complex systems of symbols, the linear narratives which frame our experience. Yet a frame invariably occults more of the world than it encompasses, and this exclusion leaves us separated from the *world-as-it-is*.

It is impossible for a human being, in a "normal" level of consciousness – that is, without explicit training or "gratuitous grace" – to experience anything of the reality of the world. Language steps in to mediate, explain, and define. The moments of ineffability are outside the bounds of human culture (if not entirely outside human experience) because at these points where language fails nothing can be known or said. This alone should tell us that while we think ourselves the masters of language, precisely the opposite is true. Language is the master of us, a tyranny from which no escape can be imagined.

This is not a new idea. The second line of the *Tao Te Ching* states the matter precisely: "The name which can be named is not the true name." In the origins of human philosophy and metaphysics, language stands out as the great interloper, separating man from the apprehension of things-as-they-are. Zen practice aims to extinguish the internal monologue, seeking a unification, a boundary dissolution between the internal state of mankind, encompassed at every point by the boundaries inherent in language, and the Absolute. This is the universal, yet entirely individual battle of mankind, the great liberation earnestly sought for. Yet, at the end, nothing is gained. And this seems reward enough, because the "mind forg'd manacles" which bind us to the world of words so hinder the progress of the soul that any release, even into Nothing, is a movement upward.

It is not as though all of us are imminently bound for Nirvana; while some will stop the Wheel of Karma, the rest will remain thoroughly entangled in the attachments of desire, hypnotically attracted to the veil of Maya. That veil is made of language; it is the seductive voice, the Siren's Call, which keeps us from our final destiny. This is bad, in that attachments produce suffering, but it is also good, a point rarely promoted by the devotees of utmost annihilation. Being in the world means being at play within the world. Without play there is no learning, without learning, no progress to the inevitable release. And in the play of the world, as in any game, there are winners and losers: there are those who skin their knees or break their bones, but at the end, everything returns to potentialities, and only the memory of having played the game remains. All of our interactions within the world leave their mark upon us, and we wage war within ourselves: we should be both naked, unadorned, and as completely transformed as the Illustrated Man, whose entire body, covered in tattoos, tells the story of his life.

In the battle between Word and Will, there are two paths, which diverge from a common entry point, and converge upon a final exit. We wish to release everything and become one with all; we wish to encompass everything and become one with all. If you desire to remove yourself from the world, there are numerous sources, starting with Lao Tze and Buddha, who can steer you in the direction of emptiness. But if you decide this is too much (or rather, too *little*) to ask, there is another path. I find the emptiness of the Absolute a bit too chilling, the light from *Ain Soph* too revealing; not because they represent the highest, but rather, because they simplify the manifold beauty. "The Tao produces one, one produces two, the two produce the three and the three produce all things."

To choose the Tao over the many things which flow from it is to assert a hierarchy of values, a violation of the very essence of the Tao. We are that river; we flow from that source. Why do we feel the need to return?

As an answer to the demands of eternal return, the French philosophers have introduced us to the idea of *forward acceleration*. When you find yourself trapped in a seemingly hopeless situation, jam your foot down on the accelerator pedal, take it to the limit, and drive straight on through to the culmination. *Immanentize the Eschaton.* What if we were to say *fine, bring it on*, and accept language for all of its enslaving faults – but, at the same time, keep a consciousness of these faults constantly before us? Where would we find ourselves? Could this lead to freedom, a freedom which is less an escape from imprisonment than an encompassing awareness that the world, with all of its traps and cages, cannot be separated from the Absolute? In any case, a recognition of the "horror of the situation" – as Gurdjieff stated it – could only put us in a better place to plot our escape. When you find yourself in the belly of the Beast, why not curl up, make yourself comfortable, and *conspire*? That most concisely describes where we are today, in an instantaneously connected, universally mediated linguistic environment of human creation. But before we conspire in any sense of safety, we must consider how language shapes the relations between human beings. Otherwise we risk exchanging the illness of linguistic infection for the cunning traps of human power.

## Rhetoric and Reason

*Good friends, sweet friends, let me not stir you up*
*To such a sudden flood of mutiny.*
*They that have done this deed are honorable:*
*What private griefs they have, alas, I know not,*
*That made them do it: they are wise and honorable,*
*And will, no doubt, with reasons answer you.*

– *Julius Caesar*, Act III, Scene 2

A few weeks before I wrote this essay, I had a private conversation with a neurophysiologist at UCSD (University of California San Diego), who passed along some stunning insights he'd gathered from his research on the human brain. It seems that although we like to perceive ourselves as rational, reasonable creatures, carefully weighing our decisions before we commit, the fact of the matter is precisely the inverse. We arrive at our decisions through emotional sensations, acting "from the gut" at all times. Our reason enters the process only after the decision has been made, and acts as the mind's propagandist, convincing us of the utter rightness which underlies all of our actions. Beyond this, reason has a social function: to convince others that our actions are correct. Friends, Romans, countrymen, lend me your ears! Not so that you can think for yourselves, but that I might instruct you in what to believe.

Thus are all the great philosophies of Socrates and Plato overturned; these men, considering themselves the paragons of reason, used their rhetorical skills to create a new tradition in thought which had nothing more behind it than the force of the words which composed it. Seen in this light, the entirety of human history becomes more farcical (and more tragic) than could possibly be imagined. Right and wrong, good and evil, these carefully argued positions are foundations built upon the shifting sands of words. The linguistic infection has left us weakened, vulnerable to a secondary, and perhaps more serious illness – conviction.

Humans are faced with a dual-headed problem; it is bad enough that the world as-we-know-it is made of words, mediated by language, and still worse that this means that other human beings can employ this condition (more precisely, conditioning) for their own ends. It likely could not be otherwise, for we are social beings; that much is encoded into our DNA and our physiology. We need for people to believe in us, to support us, to conspire with us. A human being unwillingly deprived of the society of his peers descends into madness as the fine structures of perceived reality, maintained and reinforced by the rhetorical bombardments of others' truths (and by his own, reflected back), rapidly unwind without constant reinforcement. What I tell you three times is true. What I tell you three million times is civilization.

Plato knew this: that's why he banned poets from his *Republic*. What he could not (or, more sinisterly, *would not*) recognize is that all words are poetry, rhetoric regimenting the reason. To speak and be heard means that you are sending your will out onto the world around you, changing the definition of reality for all those who hear you. We do this from the time we learn to speak (imagine the two year-old asserting his will in a shrill cry for attention, and noting a corresponding change in the behavior of those around him) till the moment we breathe our last. For most people, most of the time, this is an unconscious process, automatic and mechanical. For a few others, who, by accident or training, have become conscious of the power of reason to change men's minds, a choice is presented: *how do you use this power?*

"We are all pan-dimensional wizards, casting arcane spells with every word we speak. And every spell we speak always comes true." Owen Rowley, my mentor in both the magical mysteries and in the mysteries of virtual reality, taught me this maxim some years ago, though it took some years before I began to understand the full magnitude of his seemingly grandiose pronouncement. More than anything else, it places enormous responsibility on anyone who uses language – that is, all of us. Because we are creatures infected by language, and because language shapes how we come to interpret reality, we bear the burden of our words. We know that words can hurt, we even believe that words can kill, but the truth is far more comprehensive: all of our words are the equivalent of a hypnotist's suggestions, and all of us are to some degree susceptible. With this responsibility comes an awareness of the burden we bear. It is how we encounter this burden – as individuals and as a civilization – which shapes reality.

If power corrupts, and each of us is endowed with inestimable power, we could cast human civilization as a long war of words, a battle to determine what is real. Robert Anton Wilson once quipped, "Reality is the line where rival gangs of shamans fought to a standstill." This statement hides the fact that we're all shamans, and every time we say, "This is this," we reset the parameters of the real. Most of these shamanic battles are relatively innocent, just primate teeth-baring and jockeying for dominance in a given situation. However, in the wrong mouths, words can lead to disaster. Consider Jim Jones or Adolf Hitler, who by force of their oratory, led hundreds and millions to their deaths.

If, instead, an individual conscious of the power of words to shape the world chooses to use this power with wisdom, seeking not hegemony but liberation – a different path opens up. In this world, nothing needs to be true, and everything becomes permissible. This is the realm of conscious magick, where the realized power of the word opens possibilities for the self without constricting the potentialities of anyone else. This is the safest path, both karmically and practically; if you stay out of the way of others, there's less likelihood you'll be interfered with yourself. The magician does not proselytize; and although he may present an irresolvable paradox

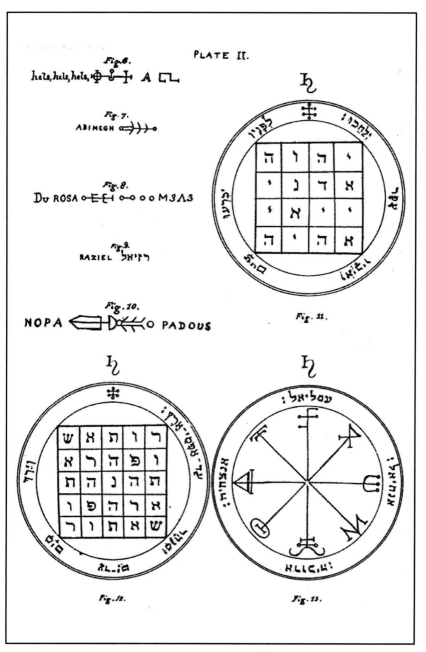

Magical 'Pentacles of Saturn', from *The Key of Solomon the King*

for those who confront his magick with their own linguistically reinforced perceptions of the world, he bares no responsibility for their reactions, nor is he susceptible to their attacks. He exists in a world apart, because there is no agreement on a common language through which a linguistic infection could spread. The magician insulates himself, inoculates himself and protects himself from the beliefs of others, while holding his own beliefs in great suspicion. Rhetoric and anti-rhetoric, combined, produces a burst of energy which propels the magician forward, with great acceleration, into a new universe of meaning.

The products of power sometimes pose too great a temptation to the magician; we have the warning tale of Faust to remind us that although the mastery of the linguistic nature of the world confers great power over others, its use inevitably leads to destruction. The magician needs a higher consciousness – in the Sufic sense – before he can toy with the wheels and dials of such power. This is why many magical orders will not initiate candidates before they have reached a certain age, or have demonstrated a material responsibility which can form a foundation from which right action can proceed. To ignore such prohibitions is to court disaster, and the checkered history of magical orders in the 19$^{th}$ and 20$^{th}$ centuries shows that far too often, ignorance has been the order of the day. Only when the magician puts down his power over others does he achieve any realizable power over himself. You are your own High Priest, and no one else's. From this everything else follows.

When the magician has arrived at this point in his path, matters of education and technique become paramount. It is very rare when an individual is granted sufficient gratuitous grace to travel on the path to wisdom entirely alone. The teacher or mentor reveals the mysteries to the initiate, but the teacher must be aware of how much the initiate can bear safely, doling out knowledge as one might dispense a powerful tonic which is also a poison. The right dosage can do great good; too much will kill. For this reason the Sufis believe that only with a "School" governed by a teacher with sufficient wisdom, can the initiate pass through the gates of wisdom.

Consider for a moment the case of John Lilly, a modern magician, who used sensory deprivation in combination with LSD-25 in a search for wisdom. He had enormous successes to begin with: *Programming and Metaprogramming in the Human Biocomputer* is one of the most effective magical texts ever published, useful for the magician throughout his training. Yet this could not keep Lilly from becoming a life-long ketamine addict, which finally left him hollowed-out and lifeless (in consensus reality), as he chose to remain in the Valley of Illusions. This is an individual choice, of course, and Lilly had his reasons (or rather, his emotions) for choosing this course for his life. But Lilly deprived himself of the opportunity for further advancement on the path of knowledge, becoming trapped within a world of chemical fantasy. His intense forward acceleration led only to a cul-de-sac, a dead-end from which he would never escape.

If such a luminary as John Lilly cannot safely pass through the gates of wisdom, what hope can be given to the aspiring magician, one who has become conscious of the power of the word to shape the world, but has no understanding of how to actualize that knowledge? We are fortunate to live in an age when all the teachings of all the ages are more or less freely available, a time when all the mysteries have been revealed. But the mysteries themselves are not enough. A community is necessary, a conspiracy of like-minded souls set on the same path, speaking the right words, words which reinforce the integrity of the self, allowing the magician to learn wisdom through a series of initiations (whether explicit or implicit), growing, like a child, into adulthood.

These do exist, and it is possible for the aspiring magician to find them without too much difficulty. Even so, a certain skepticism is necessary; "By their fruits you will know them," and although the teacher may seem overtly stern, or authoritarian, it remains up to the candidate to prepare his vessel, ready to receive illumination. Even the most profane masters can be vehicles for the illumination of their students – provided the students are properly prepared. The student must remain conscious, vigilant, and never allow the master to use linguistic traps to assign the real; that's the difference between a School and a cult.

## Word and World

*Now my charms are all o'erthrown,*
*And what strength I have's mine own*
*Which is most faint: now, 'tis true,*
*I must be here confined by you,*
*Or sent to Naples. Let me not,*
*Since I have my dukedom got*
*And pardon'd the deceiver, dwell*
*In this bare island by your spell;*
*But release me from my bands*
*With the help of your good hands.*

– *The Tempest*, Act V, Epilogue

We have by now told but half the story. Our linguistic capabilities, as employed by our reason, act upon each other to create reality. Yet beyond the reality-in-our-heads there is an exterior world (let's admit that, lest we be accused of nothing but solipsism and *word play*), which we are about to actualize as an exteriorization of our linguistic capabilities. The world presents two faces to us; the natural, that is, *that which arose by itself*, and the artificial; *that which is the product of man's interactions within the world*. While both the natural and artificial are clouded with the omnipresent linguistic fog, only the artificial world is the product of our linguistic nature. Artifacts are language concretized and exteriorized. Technology is a language of sorts, in which the forms of the world are shaped by our words, and then speak back to us. We have been throwing technological innovations into the world since we discovered fire (at least a half million years ago), and since that time the technological world, the world of artifact, has been talking back. The history of humanity, viewed in this way, can be seen as a continuous process of feedback: as we talk to the world, through our hands, the world accepts these innovations, which modify the environment within which we participate, which modifies our understanding of the world, which leads to new innovations, which modifies the environment, which modifies us, and so on, and so on. This isn't causality, or just a circling Ouroborus; this is a process, an epigenetic revolution, in which language continuously assumes a more concrete form. We are learning to talk to the hand, or rather, our hands are learning to speak, and are endowing the world of artifacts with the same linguistic infections that have so completely colonized our own biology.

This is a lot to assert, and a lot to absorb, but it is possible to approach this thesis from another point of entry, *the idea of code*. The word "code" has numerous meanings; it means one thing to a geneticist, another to a computer programmer, another to a cryptographer. Yet the underlying meaning is remarkably similar, because there is a growing sense in the scientific and technical communities that when all of the specifics are stripped away, when the very essence of the universe is revealed, it is naught but code. And what is code, precisely? Language. Whether the stepping-stairs of the amino acid base pairs which comprise the genome, or the sequence of logical steps in a computer program, or the mathematical translations which can either occult or reveal a message, code is a temporal organization of symbols – first…next…last – which establishes the basis for both operation and understanding.

The idea of the universe as code has gained great currency from mathematician Stephen Wolfram's *A New Kind of Science* (Wolfram

Media, Inc., 2002) which posits that the processes observable in the universe more often obey computational rules than algebraic formulae. He goes on to state that an enormous number of disparate processes we see in nature – the expansion of space-time, quantum interconnectedness, and the growth of biological forms – all have their basis in the fact that the universe acts as an entity which is constantly processing codes, executing programs, engaging in an execution of reality. Wolfram has been trained both as a physicist and a computer programmer; his background in both disciplines makes him uniquely qualified to identify the common ground that lies between these seemingly entirely distinct fields.

The ground seems to be rising to meet Wolfram. While biologists discover the codes of nature, physicists and chemists are applying codes to nature's most basic structures, to produce atomic-scale forms known as nanotechnology. Whether or not we choose to acknowledge it, the arrow of the epigenetic evolution of the human species points to a time in the near future when the entire world will be apprehended as code. A forthcoming "Theory of Everything" won't be a formula; it will be a *program*, a series of linguistic statements, which, like the words in a sentence, describe the execution of reality.

Here we come to the heart of the matter, where the individual apprehension of the world as linguistically conceived becomes convergent with the increasingly accepted scientific view of the universe as a linguistic process. We know that words shape the world as we see it, but now we have come to understand that words shape the world as it is. There is, at an essential level, an isomorphism between the world of the code between our ears and the reality of the code of the universe. The codes we create change our personal perceptions of the world, but they also change the world around us; the more we learn about how to modify the world, the more that language becomes convergent with reality, and the more our will extends over the real. In a real sense, beyond the narrow vision of the world underneath our skin, words are colonizing the world.

This places the magician in a unique historical position, or, rather, restores him to a position which he lost during the scientific revolution. Newton began his career as an alchemist, seeking the mystical union between man and nature which would result in the Philosopher's Stone. He did not live to see the final convergence between the language of magick and the language of science, but, more and more, science will begin to look like magick, and magicians like scientists. I don't mean this in the rude sense of *Clarke's Law* that "Any sufficiently advanced technology is indistinguishable from magic," but rather, that the principles and techniques underlying these two seemingly separate disciplines are on naturally convergent courses. The magician, master of the code, will find himself completely at home in a universe which has become linguistically apprehensible *as code*. The scientist will find himself completely at home speaking a language in which his words change the world. With the exception of those few who pursue both disciplines, neither will have noticed that they have arrived at the same point. The magician will utter his spells, the scientist will speak his codes, but both will be saying the same thing.

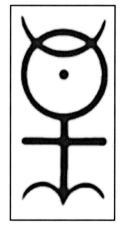

It will feel to us as though we have come full circle. The ancients of the West compiled grimoires, magical texts which presented the lessons learned by generations of practitioners in a series of spells, linguistic incantations which used the word to shape the will. Aboriginal cultures wove these lessons into "songlines", expressing the mythic narrative of culture as the infinite possibility beyond consensus reality, a "dreamtime". Now, knowing the ground for the first time, we are using our gifts with language – in genetics and informatics and chemistry – to speak the word, and make the world. The idea of code is overflowing, becoming the world itself, and reality will soon be as programmable as the writer's page, responding to the will of the magician like some lucid dream. In this executable dreamtime everything is true, within limits determined by experiment; once those limits are known, a new generation of magicians will undoubtedly attempt to transcend them.

What will this world look like? We have no precedent in profane history to use as a guide; we must look further afield, to mythology, to understand the form of a linguistic universe. It is the dreamtime of the Aboriginal Australians, or the Faeire of the Celts, the absolute expansion of possibilities – both angelic and demonic – in that everything expressible can be brought into being. The masters of linguistic intent in both magical and scientific forms (a false distinction) will be masters of word and world. *Say the word, and it will come to pass.*

Although this process appears inevitable, it could be that we are bound by the same "Single Vision and Newton's Sleep" that William Blake prophesied 200 years ago. It could be that the universe is not code, but simply that the idea of code has overflowed from our brain's linguistic centers into other areas of the cerebrum, colonizing our reason and intellectual capabilities as easily as it captured our ability to apprehend sequence. This could all be a chimera, an elusive possibility which may remain tantalizingly out of reach. Yet the whole world seems to be conspiring to teach us this: *In the beginning was the word.*

**Mark Pesce** is an inventor, writer, teacher, broadcaster and entrepreneur. The author of six books – including THE NEXT BILLION SECONDS (nextbillionseconds.com) – he has been studying the close relationship between *ontos* (being) and *techne* (doing) for a quarter of a century.

*The Executable Dreamtime*

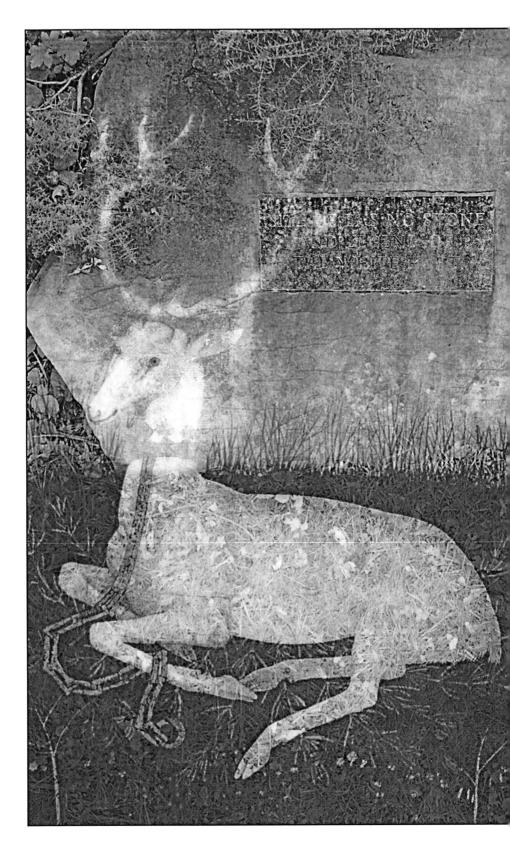

# The Hunting of the White Hart

## NEW INSIGHTS INTO AN ANCIENT MYTHIC THEME

by *Richard Andrews*

The legend of Herne the Hunter, an antlered figure associated with an old stag-horned oak which once stood in Windsor Great Park, is a tale much-referenced by modern pagans who perceive, in its earliest literary forms, the signs of an oral tradition, the origins of which stretch back into the unfathomed depths of prehistory.

This strange story is one of many tales, told across Europe, of a Wild Huntsman who typically, in pursuit of a ghostly white stag or hart across the skies, leads a noisy band of unbaptised (i.e. pagan) souls to the Otherworld. Apparent sightings of the spectral Wild Hunt were often taken as a sign of an imminent death, and in the case of Herne in particular, that of a king or direct heir to the Crown.

Herne has much in common with Woden, the chief god of the Anglo-Saxons, sometimes known as 'the stag', who hung himself on the world tree, and was also remembered as a leader of the Wild Hunt. He also exhibits many characteristics of the archetypal pagan 'horned god' (demoted to devilish status by Christianity), sometimes dubbed Cernunnos. As the Lord of the Forest, the divine ruler of wild nature, Cernunnos appears in the form of a stag, or wearing antlers and is guardian of, and guide to, the Otherworld.

The Wild Hunt is particularly associated with midnight and midwinter, and often appears during the twelve nights of Christmas. It is sometimes said to be seen at the equinoxes, solstices and cross-quarter days celebrated by pagan festivities. In the Roman Catholic world it commonly desecrates church festivals such as Lent, Good Friday, or the eve of St Walpurga's Day (May 1st).

The earliest literary reference to the legend of Herne the Hunter was by Shakespeare in his play *The Merry Wives of Windsor*, first performed in 1597, and published in 1602.

> *There is an old tale goes, that Herne the hunter,*
> *Sometime a keeper here in Windsor Forest*
> *Doth all the winter-time, at still midnight,*
> *Walk round about an oak, with great ragg'd horns,*
> *And there he blasts the tree, and takes the cattle,*
> *And makes milch-kine yield blood, and shakes a chain,*
> *In a most hideous and dreadful manner.*
> *You have heard of such a spirit, and well you know,*
> *The superstitious idle-headed eld,*
> *Receiv'd, and did deliver to our age,*
> *This tale of Herne the Hunter for a truth.*

However, the best-known version of the legend appears in a novel by William Harrison Ainsworth, *Windsor Castle* (1843).[1] Ainsworth's version was undoubtedly partly influenced by Shakespeare, but it is widely thought to reveal traces of local oral tradition because of the many recognisable pagan mythical themes to be found in the tale. These would appear to be too well integrated within Ainsworth's romance to be accounted for by the author's own potential knowledge of pagan mythology.[2]

My aim in this essay is to demonstrate how a clue in the legend of Herne the Hunter, relating to a previously-overlooked territorial aspect of its mythical roots, impacts the debate around the legend's origins. In so doing, I identify a local place-based legend, not previously explored in the context of the legend of Herne the Hunter and its wider mythic theme. Before that, I'll give a brief overview of the legend as it appears in Ainsworth's novel, then introduce the mythic theme of the 'Hunting of the White Hart' and its application to the art of Medieval kingship.

## The Legend of Herne the Hunter

The story goes that Richard II was out hunting when, in pursuit of a large stag, he and Herne, his most talented royal huntsman, broke away from the hunting party. As they closed in on the wounded beast, it turned and unseated the king from his horse. Herne intervened, taking the blows of the stag's antlers in the king's stead, and dispatched the stag with a knife through its throat despite receiving a life-threatening wound in this act of self-sacrifice. In return for saving his life, the king promised to Herne the head keepership of Windsor Forest, with lodgings at the castle, should he survive.

When the king offered a reward to whomever could save Herne, a tall, dark, strangely-dressed man, who had joined the hunt unseen, came forward, giving the name of Phil Urswick. With the king's permission, Urswick had Herne crowned with the dead stag's antlered skull and carried to his hut in the wildest part of Bagshot Heath. However, as Herne's fellow huntsmen were jealous of the prospect of his survival and promotion, the wizardly Urswick took advantage by offering to deprive the new head keeper of his hunting skill, though in return for an unspecified future request.

Though he survived, Herne – deprived of his hunting skills by Urswick – was inevitably dismissed from his promised post. Offered a week's leave by the king, he rode off into the forest and later reappeared in a crazed state, wearing the stag skull. Soon after, a pedlar found him hanging from an oak tree in the forest, but all the keepers found was the rope. That evening, somewhat portentously, the oak was struck by lightning.

When each successor to the post of keeper inherited the debilitating curse, Urswick directed the huntsmen to Herne's Oak, and when Herne's spirit appeared, he commanded the party to take Herne as their leader. Every night they hunted the king's deer until, when the king found out, he confronted Herne at his oak. It was agreed that Herne would cease haunting/hunting the forest for the remainder of the king's reign, if the other hunters would hang for their part in his downfall. Herne's hunt has been reportedly seen in the forest many times since, especially at times of national crisis.

Herne the Hunter, as depicted by George Cruikshank

## The Hunting of the White Hart

The stag has a rich symbolic meaning. The noted authority on symbols J.C. Cooper's statement[3] that "Following the hunted deer or stag often leads to symbolic situations, and the stag can also be a messenger of the gods or heavenly powers", is exemplified by the legend of Saint Hubert. Hubert (of Merovingian lineage, a royal bloodline said to be descended from Jesus) was a keen hunter who, upon his wife's death during childbirth, lost himself in the worldly pleasures of hunting and turned away from religion. Then one Good Friday morning, the great stag he was pursuing turned to reveal a crucifix between its antlers, whereupon he heard these words: "Hubert, unless thou turnest to the Lord, and leadest an holy life, thou shalt quickly go down into hell". Hubert's story is essentially a Christian overlay on the common theme of the stag hunt in pagan myth. He even appears in French tradition as a leader of the Wild Hunt, and his feast day, on November 3rd, is suspiciously close to Hallowe'en.

For the Celts the white stag was an otherworldly messenger or psychopomp, a leader of souls to the realm of Faery. The common Celtic/Arthurian mythic scenario of the young hero or prince who is inspired to go hunting and becomes disoriented as he is led deeper into the forest in pursuit of a white stag is a classic 'call to adventure', announcing the beginning of an otherworldly quest. A similar scenario can be found in Germanic tradition, in which Odin hunts a stag which lures him to the mansion of Queen Hulda.

As a recurring mythic theme in dynastic legends, the hunting of the white hart is a test of the hero's fitness to be king, to be the consort of the queen as representative of the Goddess of Sovereignty. By hunting down this 'King of the Forest', a symbol of regal status, the king symbolically affirms his authority.[4] In Irish myth, according to John Grenham,[5] "the legitimacy of the ruling house is confirmed when a stag enters; the animal is hunted, and the border of the territory is defined by the chase; the future ruler is the individual who eventually slays the stag."

One early Irish legend tells how the pre-Gaelic King Dáire named all five of his sons Lugaid, after his druid prophesied that a son of his so named would gain the kingship of the whole of Ireland. To find out which it was to be, Dáire is told that a fawn with a golden lustre on its fur would enter the assembly at Tailtiu and the son who catches it would win the kingship. Upon its appearance, the sons chase the fawn to Benn Étair (the Hill of Howth), the easternmost point of Ireland, where a magical mist descends and the sons of Dáire become separated from the rest of the hunters. (This is the edge of the land and the boundary between the worlds.) Lugaid Loígde then catches the fawn. During a second bout of hunting, the brothers encounter an old hag during a snowstorm, who challenges them to sleep with her in return for a bed and sustenance. When Lugaid Loígde alone accepts her offer, she is transformed into a beautiful maiden and announces that he has won the sovereignty of the land.

A Welsh example of sovereignty myth is the tale of Pwyll, Prince of Dyfed. Pwyll, in the now familiar manner, loses his companions while out on a hunt. On seeing an otherworldly pack of hounds bearing down on a stag, he sets his own hounds after it. He then encounters Arawn (perhaps etymologically related to Herne), a king of the Otherworld (Annwn), mounted on a horse. To appease Arawn for his transgression, Pwyll agrees to exchange identities with Arawn, and takes his place for a year and a day (the traditional initiation period) in the Otherworld, where (besides behaving honourably towards Arawn's queen) he defeats Arawn's enemy Havgan, king of a neighbouring realm, on his final day, thereby earning the title 'Pen Annwn' (Head of the Otherworld). The battle between Pwyll (standing in for Arawn) and Havgan invites interpretation in terms of the cycle of the seasons, the eternal battle between the Lords of Winter and Summer. While a single blow from Pwyll could have killed Havgan (and a second blow revive him), in the event, Pwyll

merely wounds Havgan, but wins the battle, thus uniting the two otherworldly kingdoms.

The same hunting theme appears in Arthurian legend, wherein it was said that whoever hunted down a white hart could claim a kiss from the most beautiful girl in Arthur's court. For example, in "Eric and Enide", by Chretien de Troyes:

> *On Easter day, in springtime,*
> *at Cardigan, his castle,*
> *King Arthur held court.*
> *So rich a one was ever seen,*
> *for there were many good knights,*
> *brave and combative and fierce,*
> *and rich ladies and maidens,*
> *daughters of kings, noble and beautiful;*
> *but before the court concluded*
> *the king said to his knights*
> *that he wanted to hunt the white stag*
> *in order to revive the tradition.*
> *My lord Gawain was not a bit pleased*

*when he heard this:*
*"Sire," said he, "from this hunt*
*you will never have either gratitude nor thanks.*
*We have all known for a long time*
*what tradition is attached to the white stag:*
*he who can kill the white stag*
*by right must kiss*
*the most beautiful of the maidens of your court,*
*whatever may happen."*

Of the white hart in Arthurian legend, Caitlin Matthews states:

> Its appearance marks the assumption by Arthur of a ritual role, as the Huntsman consort of Sovereignty, whose beast the White Hart is… [T]he White Hart's head is awarded to the most beautiful maiden, from whom Arthur is expected to exact a kiss, a token of a more explicit surrender which the Spring Maiden once rendered to the Huntsman King.[6]

## Medieval Kingship

As we pass from Celtic 'legend' to medieval 'history', we find several accounts of British kings hunting, and threatened by, a stag whilst establishing their territorial claims against a rival. As I have discovered, the idea that 'the border of the territory is defined by the chase', when applied to these legends, explains much of their detail, the significance of which has not previously been recognised, as far as I am aware.

David I of Scotland was said to have been saved from a charging white stag, after being thrown from his horse during a chase, on the Feast Day of the Holy Rood (the cross of Christ) in 1127. When he grasped the huge beast's antlers and pleaded for divine intervention, he had a vision of the cross, and the stag fled. He commemorated the miracle in 1228 by founding an Abbey on the site, dedicated to the Holy Rood, which became the nucleus of Holyrood Palace, the seat of the Scottish monarchy in Edinburgh.

In the context of David's questionable claim to the whole Scottish kingdom, after his brother Alexander I of Scotland died in 1124, and his ten-year struggle to subdue his rival and nephew Máel Coluim mac Alaxandair to the north of his southern Principality of the Cumbrians, David's act of foundation, presumably on the edge of the territory he now controlled, made good sense.

A legend associated with the founder of the Clan McKenzie, one Colin FitzGerald who, tradition records, was a member of the House of Geraldine in Ireland, tells that he risked his life to save the Scottish King Alexander III from a charging stag, which he shot with a single arrow, in 1263. The grateful king granted him the lands of Kintail. History tells us that this was the year after Alexander's minority ended, and in which King Haakon of Norway invaded the Western Isles after rejecting Alexander's claim over them. FitzGerald, who had settled in Scotland with many followers several years earlier, was instrumental in repelling the invasion.

When, according to legend, Henry III hunted down a white hart in the medieval forest of Blackmore in Dorset, he saved the animal, and fitted it with a brass collar on which was engraved "I am a royal hart, let no one harm me". But on his refusal to make good the damage caused to the land of one Thomas de la Linde, the latter gentleman hunted and killed the white hart, thus incurring imprisonment and an annual tax called 'White Hart Silver'.

Looking closely at the legend of Herne the Hunter, we find that, according to Ainsworth's retelling of the legend, Richard II's stag-slaying (by proxy, thanks to Herne) occurred "within a few miles of Hungerford, whither the borders of the forest then extended". Hungerford, it turns out, was the manor of the Duke of Lancaster, John of Gaunt, Richard's uncle, who effectively ruled England during Richard's minority. Once his minority was over, Richard would have wanted to put Gaunt in his place. It looks like this part of the tale can also be read as political allegory – a symbolic reaffirmation of Richard's sovereignty over (and his keeper's earned stewardship of) the Royal Forest.

When John died, Richard confiscated his property, but Gaunt's exiled son Henry Bolingbroke (soon to be Henry IV) took advantage of Richard's absence while on campaign in Ireland, and with the support of the barons, deposed Richard (who died mysteriously in prison), and triggered the dynastic Wars of the Roses. The Wars were eventually resolved by the Lancastrian claimant (Henry VII)'s marriage to the Yorkist heiress. It comes as no surprise now that there is a story which tells how Henry VII caught a white hart at Ringwood – at the bounds of the New Forest both literally and physically – gave it a golden leash (and the name 'Albert'!) and a crown as a collar (thus marking it as the property of the crown), and took it to Windsor Forest.

Significantly, Ringwood had been owned by the 'Kingmaker' Richard, Earl of Warwick, the richest and most powerful peer of his time, who was instrumental in bringing to power Edward IV and Henry VI – the latter after a failed plot to crown Edward's brother, George, Duke of Clarence. After Richard died in battle in 1471, Ringwood passed to his daughter Isabel, wife of George, who was executed in 1478 for plotting against his brother. After the death of Isabel, and during her son's minority, the stewardship of the manor was eventually given to the king's servant John Hoton in 1484. Ringwood thus passed to the Crown, to be taken by Henry VII the next year.

The ancient origin of the hunting of the white hart is confirmed by Aristotle, who relates how Agathocles, a King of Sicily, killed a white stag consecrated to Diana by Diomedes a thousand years before. Pliny recorded that Alexander the Great caught a white stag, placed a gold collar around its neck and set it free. Later stories place Julius Caesar and Charlemagne in this role. The Roman writer Solinus states that white stags found 300 years after Caesar's death had collars inscribed with *"Noli me tangere, Caesaris sum"* ("Touch me not, for I am Caesar's").

These legends of medieval kings, symbolically defending the bounds of their Royal Forests, call to mind the *Rex Nemorensis*, who stood guard over Diana's sacred grove at Nemi (as priest and consort of the virgin goddess of the hunt), having earned his position by plucking a golden bough from one of the trees in the grove before slaying the previous incumbent. This 'King of the Wood' was at the heart of James Frazer's classical study, The Golden Bough,[7] an interpretation of myth in terms of sacred kingship, as a reenactment of pagan fertility rites. To Frazer, the *Rex Nemorensis* was an expression of a universal mythic archetype, of a sacred king who was periodically sacrificed as the representative of the dying and resurrected vegetation god.

Like the pagan legends from which they are derived, these tales of medieval kingship serve to reinforce the ancient idea that the fate of a king is intimately bound up with that of his land. The dangerous stag is a symbol of the rival forces the king must overcome when founding or defending his kingdom, and a reminder that a wounded king represents a vulnerable kingdom.

Whether certain elements of the legend of Herne the Hunter derive from traces of local oral tradition, or from Victorian romance, remains a matter of debate. But the significant location of the hunt's climax, in the demonstrated context of the consistent and deliberate exploitation of pagan sovereignty myth for political purposes in medieval times, presumably a large part of its function from time immemorial, suggests that much of the local detail in the legend derives from a medieval makeover in the reign of Richard II.

The anthropologist Margaret Murray put forward the idea, based on James Frazer's work, that the concept of divine kingship (viewing a king as an incarnation or agent of deity) survived into medieval times as part of a witch-cult.[8] In support of her hypothesis, for example, she interpreted the shooting of William II in 1100, during a hunt in the New Forest, by an arrow supposedly meant for a stag, as evidence of William's divine kingship. Many scholars regard the possibility of his assassination as a credible scenario, his brother and successor Henry having been present at the hunt. While the witch-cult idea remains a popular myth in parts of the neopagan community, it has been roundly rejected by historians on grounds of a lack of evidence.

That is not to say that the idea of divine kingship did not survive in a Christian context. That Christianity was uncomfortable with the unchristian origins of the theme of the royal stag hunt is made clear in the legends associated with Saint Hubert and David I, in which the hunt takes place on the taboo date of a Christian Holy Day, but a Christian religious vision saves the day, as it were.

## The Basing Stone

Richard II's personal emblem of the white hart, derived from his mother's arms, was an overt sign of his devotion to the ancient model of divine kingship. The white hart is depicted on the Wilton Diptych, a portable altarpiece before which Richard would pray. The front shows Jesus, in Mary's arms, passing a pennant bearing the cross of St George, symbol of the sovereignty of England, to the kneeling

Site of the Basing Stone and Legend of the White Hart

Richard. On the orb atop the staff is depicted a white castle on an island, approached by a ship. While it is thought that this island could represent Britain, it also resembles a symbolic otherworldly scene from the Grail legends and earlier Celtic works. It recalls, for instance, the marble castle by a harbour, to which the hero of *Guigemar* (based on a Breton story and attributed to Marie de France) sails. From this castle, he rescues the lady who becomes his lover, and who heals him of the thigh-wound he suffered while hunting, from an arrow rebounding off the head of a fatally-injured white hind.

A little-known local Surrey legend, echoing the key event in the legend of Herne, tells how a white hart once protected Richard from a wounded stag.[9] Richard is said to have commemorated the event by having four inns with the sign of the White Hart built at Bagshot, Frimley, Chobham and Pirbright. (It was Richard who, in 1389, passed an Act requiring pubs and inns to display a sign to aid their identification by the official Ale Taster, and many were named "The White Hart" after Richard's heraldic emblem.)

The site of this encounter, 'near the Basing Stone', is on Bagshot's western parish boundary, where it is crossed by the Great South West Road from London to Land's End (A30), at its junction with the Portsmouth Road (A325). Might this also be the legendary location of the wizard's hut in which Herne was healed and which Harrison Ainsworth placed in the midst of Bagshot Heath? Another version of the legend simply states that a white hart with a collar was once found by the stone.

Sadly, the stone which stands there today is a replacement for the original, which was apparently destroyed during road widening in the 1950s. Perhaps it served as a milestone, getting its name from the parish of Old Basing, fifteen miles to the southwest, along the A30. Another theory is that it was a boundary marker for land held by a Robert de Basing in 1218, originally granted by Henry II out of his demesne lands within the Forest (the terms of tenure being to provide the king with a leash of hounds). As such, it would have marked the boundary of Windsor Forest, a possibility which is only fitting with its interpretation as a sacred marker of royal territory, as suggested by its associated legend.

It is interesting, from a symbolic perspective, that the characteristics of the Basing Stone echo those of Ancient Greek Hermai. Sacred to Hermes, these were phallic stone pillars, serving as boundary markers, way markers or milestones at crossroads or street corners. They functioned as ritual site guardians, warding off evil spirits at places of transition. Hermes is the god of gateways, boundaries and crossings, "responsible for the safety of all divine property". He is a patron and protector of merchants, thieves and travellers, his duties including "the maintenance of free rights of way for travellers on any road in the world".[10] As the personification of liminality or boundary-crossing, Hermes is the trickster of the Ancient Greek pantheon. He is a messenger between realms, and as Hermes Psychopompos, a guide of souls to the otherworld. Both Hermes and Woden reveal wisdom through the interpretation of signs, and both were identified by the Romans with Mercury. In alchemy, the elusive, metamorphosing Mercurial spirit is known as *cervus fugitivus*, the fugitive stag. Herne, as a leader of the Wild Hunt, can also be considered a psychopomp. His reputed appearance at liminal moments, and his ambiguous form, which blurs the boundary between the hunter and the hunted, reveals his trickster aspect.

The Basing Stone, or rather its gravestone, memorialises the site of Richard II's legendary hunt, standing as a symbolic marker of the threshold between this mortal world and the immortal otherworld, whose representatives are the wounded stag and the white hart.

**Richard Andrews** is a freelance web professional and aspiring author. He has studied environmental psychology at postgraduate level and has a Diploma in Heritage Interpretation. Some of you may know him as Daily Grail admin 'Perceval'.

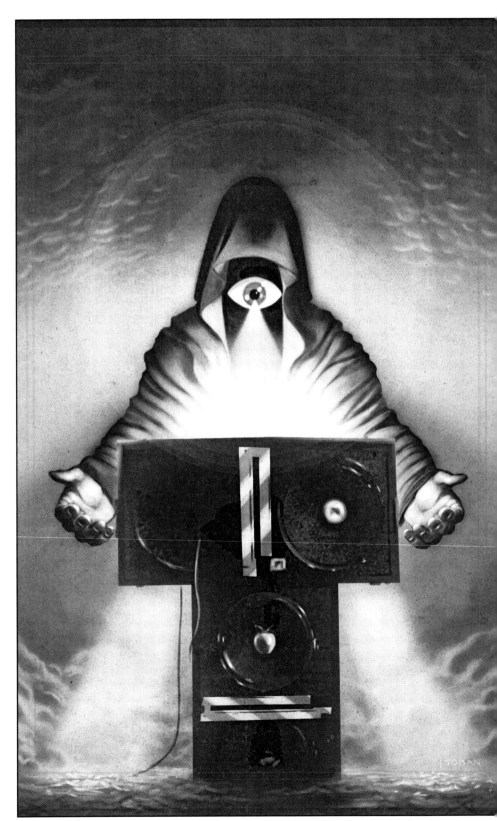

# From
# OPERATION MINDF\*\*K
## to
# THE WHITE ROOM

## The Strange Discordian Journey of The KLF

by *J.M.R. Higgs*

In the 1980s, pop stars made movies. Prince, Madonna and the Pet Shop Boys all went in front of the cameras. The KLF made a film as well, but they went about it in a very different manner. Theirs was never released, or even properly finished, and they made it before they had a string of hit singles rather than afterwards. It was called *The White Room*.

*The White Room* is a very different beast to *Purple Rain* or *Desperately Seeking Susan*. It's a dialogue-free ambient road movie just under an hour in length, for a start. The band had experimented with ambient film before, shooting an experimental movie called *Waiting* on VHS on the Isle of Jura the previous year. *The White Room*, however, had been shot with a professional crew and cost around £250,000, money they had earned from a Doctor Who-themed novelty record they had released under the name The Timelords.

The film starts at a rave in the basement of a South London squat known as Transcentral. Bill Drummond and Jimmy Cauty, the duo behind The KLF, leave the party and get into a 1968 Ford Galaxie American police car. In the back sits a solicitor, played by their own solicitor David Franks. He hands them a contract, which the pair sign without reading. Franks exits and Drummond and Cauty drive off.

Pretty much most of the rest of the film is them driving.

First, they drive around London at night. Then, they drive around the Sierra Nevada region of Spain. This goes on for some time. Not much happens, although they do find a dead eagle, and at one point they stop for petrol.

Eventually the pair stop and build a camp fire, an event which occurs twice in the film. At each point, the solicitor is seen in the smoke from the fire, studying the contract – a distinctly Faustian image. The solicitor discovers something in one of the contract's clauses, and writes 'Liberation Loophole!' on the contract.

Events in the film now gain more momentum. Drummond is seen throwing the contract into the air, obviously delighted. He has, by this point, changed into a pair of plus-fours and is dressed not unlike an Edwardian mountaineer. Cauty then paints the car white and they drive, past a burning bush, up into the snow-peaked mountains. When the car gets stuck in the snow they abandon it and continue up on foot. Cauty has not joined Drummond in sporting the Edwardian mountaineer look, instead wearing a more sensible white parka. Eventually they reach the summit, where they find a large white building with a radio telescope. They go in.

They find themselves in a white, smoke-filled void – the White Room. They find a pair of fake moustaches on a pedestal, and put them on. Then they find the solicitor, sitting at a white table. He shows them the clause he has found in the contract. They nod. The pair then walk away, dissolving into the smoke and vanishing into the void. The End.

It was, all in all, an odd way to spend £250,000. The story of why it was made, however, is far stranger.

## The Most Influential Photocopier in History?

In the mid-1960s a photocopier was state of the art technology, and having access to one was something of a privilege. The act of using an office photocopier after hours for personal projects, without the boss knowing, was therefore a far riskier and more rebellious act than it is today. This was certainly the case for Lane Caplinger, a secretary for New Orleans District Attorney Jim Garrison.

In 1991 Garrison was portrayed by Kevin Costner in Oliver Stone's movie *JFK*, a film based on Garrison's book *On The Trail Of The Assassins*. But this was 1965, a year before he became involved in Kennedy conspiracies and two years before the Summer of Love thrust hippies, psychedelic drugs and alternative lifestyles in front of an unprepared public. Things had not yet begun to 'get weird', in other words, and for a respected public figure like Garrison, there was little to indicate what surprises the future had in store. He would have been quite unprepared, then, for the book that Caplinger and her friend Greg Hill were clandestinely producing in his office.

This book was the original version of what would become known as the *Principia Discordia*, or *How I Found The Goddess and What I Did To Her When I Found Her*, by a writer named Malaclypse the Younger. They made a first edition of five copies. At the time it was little more than a joke for some of their friends, but its influence is now scrawled in a haphazard, and frequently illegible, manner across the history of the late twentieth century.

There was some debate in the 1970s, when the book's influence began to spread, as to just who this 'Malaclypse the Younger' was.

Some believed that the book was the work of Timothy Leary. Others claimed it was written by Alan Watts, or by Richard Nixon during "a few moments of lucidity". It is now generally accepted that the book was largely the work of Caplinger's friend Greg Hill, although large chunks were also written by Hill's old school friend Kerry Thornley.

The ideas behind the book can be traced back to the late 1950s, when Hill and Thornley attended California High School in East Whittier, a rural Southern Californian town that was then nestled amongst vast orange groves. In school they were viewed as nerds. Hill was short, squat and introverted, while Thornley was tall, very thin, and bursting with a nervous energy. They both shared an enthusiasm for pranks and strange ideas. They were also both keen on bowling alleys, largely because they served alcohol and remained open until two in the morning.

It was in one such bowling alley in 1957 that Thornley showed Hill some poetry that he was writing. It included a reference to order eventually arising out of chaos. Hill laughed at this. He told Thornley that the idea of 'order' was an illusion. Order is just something that the human mind projects onto reality. What really exists behind this fake veneer is an infinite, churning chaos. For Hill, an atheist, the failure to understand this was the major folly of the organised religions of the world, all of which claim that there is an organising principle at work in the Universe.

Hill also told Thornley that the Greeks were an exception to this rule, as they had had a Goddess of Chaos. Her name was Eris, which meant 'strife' and which is translated as 'Discordia' in Latin. Clearly, if anyone wanted to worship a deity who could be considered real, in that they were genuinely and unarguably active in this world, then Eris was the only sensible option. All that was needed was for someone to create a religion around Her which, naturally, they decided to do. They called it Discordianism.

Slowly Hill and Thornley recruited a few like-minded friends into their new religion. Their aim was to undermine existing belief systems by spreading confusion and disinformation with as much humour as possible. To this end they each adopted a host of new names under which their Discordian endeavours were credited. Hill became known varyingly as Malaclypse the Younger, Rev. Dr. Occupant, Mad Malik, Ignotum P. Ignotious or Professor Iggy. Thornley became Omar Khayyam Ravenhurst, Rev. Jesse Sump, Ho Chi Zen or the Bull Goose of Limbo. Many different Discordian chapters were founded – the majority of which contained only one member, and some contained none. Discordians would then write essays and letters under these aliases, only to then follow them with completely contradictory essays and letters under a different alias. Gradually this process spread and, by the time it reached its height in the late Sixties and early Seventies, it had become known as Operation Mindfuck. The aim of Operation Mindfuck was to lead people into such a heightened state of bewilderment and confusion that their rigid beliefs would shatter and be replaced by some form of enlightenment.

Eris

That was the aim, anyway. In practice it rarely worked out so well, with those heavily absorbed in Discordianism proving as likely to succumb to paranoid schizophrenia as to any form of enlightenment.

Discordianism is often described as being either an elaborate satire disguised as a religion or an elaborate religion described as a satire, a description which wrongly assumes that it cannot be both at the same time. It certainly was a joke, of course, at least to start with. The whole concept was an atheist satire or, at most, a way to deal with nihilism by wrapping it up with a Goddess and a sense of humour. As events unfurled and strange synchronicities began to stack up, however, it became harder and harder to claim that what was going on was 'just' a joke.

For those early Discordians it became increasingly tempting to believe that when Greg Hill used D.A. Garrison's photocopier to produce the first edition of *Principia Discordia*, something, some spirit of Discord and Chaos, emerged, or returned, or arrived in the world we know. Of course, Greg Hill was an atheist who intended Discordianism to be a satire of religion. He certainly did not start out taking the idea of Goddesses or spirits seriously. By the late 70s, however, he was convinced that his Discordian adventures had stirred up something that he was unable to explain. As he told his friend Margot Adler:

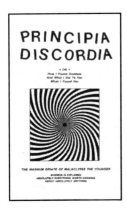

If you do this type of thing well enough, it starts to work. I started out with the idea that all gods are an illusion. By the end I had learned that it is up to you to decide whether gods exist, and if you take the goddess of confusion seriously enough, it will send you through as profound and valid a metaphysical trip as taking a god like Yahweh [the Jewish/Christian/Muslim God] seriously.

The effects of invoking a made-up god, in other words, were no different to sincerely invoking a 'proper' one. This was going to be an eventful realization for those that invoked Eris. As Thornley once remarked to Hill, "You know, if I had realised that all of this was going to come *true*, I'd have chosen Venus."

## Jung of Mind

The psychologist Carl Jung credited a particular dream as being a turning point in his life, one which convinced him to embark on the study of synchronicity and the subconscious. He wrote about this dream in his book *Memories, Dreams, Reflections*. In due course the Liverpudlian poet Peter O'Hallighan read about the dream in that book, and came to view it with equal significance. In his dream, Jung found himself…

> …in a dark, sooty city. It was night, and winter, and dark, and raining. I was in Liverpool. With a number of Swiss – say half a dozen – I walked through the dark streets.

Like many scousers, O'Hallighan's home city was a significant part of his personal identity, so Jung's mention of Liverpool immediately grabbed him. In later years, he researched Jung's life in an effort to discover if there was a link that explained the setting of Liverpool in this dream. But he did not find any. Jung had never been to Liverpool, and didn't have any obvious connection to the place.

Jung's account of his dream continued:

> It reminded me of Basel, where the market is down below and you go up through the Tottengässchen (Alley of the Dead), which leads to a plateau above and so to the Petersplatz and the Peterskirche.
>
> …When we reached the plateau, we found a broad square, dimly illuminated by street lights, into which many streets converged. The various quarters of the city were arranged radially around the square.

The 'Peter' in the street names gave Peter O'Hallighan a personal connection to the dream, and inspired him to search Liverpool for the best candidate for the "broad square" mentioned. He came to believe that Jung was referring to the square at the end of Matthew Street. This was an area that then consisted of old warehouses between the centre of the city and the waterfront, and was also the exact same place where O'Hallighan had recently leased a building. Some years after Jung's dream one of these warehouses would become a club called the Cavern, from where the Beatles would emerge to change the world.

Jung continued:

In the centre was a round pool, and in the middle of it, a small island. While everything around was obscured by rain, fog, smoke and dimly lit darkness, the little island blazed with sunlight. On it stood a single tree, a magnolia, in a sea of reddish blossoms. It was as though the tree stood in the sunlight and was, at the same time, the source of light. My companions commented on the abominable weather, and obviously did not see the tree. They spoke of another Swiss who was living in Liverpool, and expressed surprise that he should have settled here. I was carried away by the beauty of the tree and the sunlit island, and thought, "I know very well why he has settled here." Then I awoke.

Jung felt that his subconscious had shown him something of profound importance. "Everything was extremely unpleasant, black and opaque – just as I felt then", he wrote. "But I had had a vision of unearthly beauty, and that was why I was able to live at all. Liverpool is the 'pool of life'. The 'liver', according to an old view, is the seat of life - that which 'makes to live'." Jung had found, bubbling up from his subconscious, an image that inspired him. It was no more than a dream image, but it was more powerful and had a greater impact on him than things which physically exist.

Jung's dream had a profound effect on O'Hallighan because he too had had a dream. He had dreamt that he saw a spring bubbling forth from a cast-iron drain cover in the middle of the road where Matthew Street, Button Street and others converge. He came down to Matthew Street the next day and sure enough, there was a manhole cover where he had dreamt one. He also saw that one remaining warehouse had a 'To Let' sign outside. He had then gone to the bank, got a loan and leased the building. He turned the downstairs into a market, and opened a café above it. The market became known as Aunt Twackies, a pun on the scouse mispronunciation of 'antiques' as 'an teek wees'. He would later discover that there was an ancient spring underneath the building, which fed into an old brick-built reservoir.

When he later read of Jung's dream, he was struck by the way that Jung seemed to have dreamt of the exact same location, and that he too had linked it to some elemental source of life. This seemed deeply significant to O'Hallighan. He arranged for a bust of Jung to be placed in the outside wall.

## Marching to the Beat of a Different Drummond

The market began to attract members of the local music scene due to its proximity to Probe Records and Eric's nightclub, and because they could spend a day talking and planning in the café for the price of a cup of tea. One of the regulars was Bill Drummond, then 23 years old. Drummond was working as a set builder at the Everyman theatre having returned to Liverpool, where he had attended college, after spending some time working on the trawler boats in his native Scotland. One day he wandered in and found O'Hallighan hammering a nail into a piece of wood. O'Hallighan told him that he was planning to open what he called the 'Liverpool School of Language, Music, Dream and Pun'. He also told him about Jung's dream. "I didn't really understand what O'Hallighan was on about", Drummond recalled later, "but it resonated and I remembered it almost word for word."

The Liverpool School of Language, Music, Dream and Pun was planning on staging plays. O'Hallighan had persuaded the actor and director Ken Campbell to base his next project there. This was quite a coup, as Campbell's previous touring show, *The Ken Campbell Roadshow*, had been something of a success. It had featured Campbell, together with a troop of actors including Bob Hoskins and Sylvester McCoy, dramatizing weird and wonderful 'friend of a friend' stories. The reason why O'Hallighan wanted to stage plays was, naturally enough, another one of his dreams. This dream had featured a building with a raging fire upstairs and a play being performed in a theatre in the basement. Strangely, there was a copy of *Playboy* magazine on a seat in the theatre, and though this didn't immediately make much sense, in the dream it seemed in some way significant…

## From Playboy to the Illuminati

The editors of the *Playboy* letter pages during the mid-Sixties were Robert Anton Wilson and Bob Shea. In many ways their jobs were not that different to most office jobs, except that the secretaries tended to be prettier, and every week or so they'd be invited up to Hugh Hefner's mansion to "watch movies and stuff". A lot of the reader letters they received, though, were decidedly odd.

In part this was because some of these were from the small, initial group of Discordians, and the two Bobs found themselves in frequent letter communication with Kerry Thornley. They soon became committed Discordians themselves, with Wilson adopting the Discordian name Mordecai the Foul and Shea calling himself Josh the Dill. It was not long before the *Playboy* forum took on, under these two editors, a decidedly weird turn. Many letters proclaimed deeply complicated and contradictory conspiracy theories. The strange thing was, though, that they weren't writing them all themselves. Whilst many could be attributed to their small core of Discordian colleagues, there were many others which appeared to be from complete strangers. Or were they? This was a problem with Operation Mindfuck, as you couldn't trust your friends to be honest about their activities. But still, judging by factors such as the postmarks on letters and unknown handwriting, there appeared to be many conspiratorial letters arriving from people that they didn't know. The Discordian ideas, which Thornley had been spreading in printed handbills and, eventually, in the *Principia Discordia*, were starting to spread. And they were spreading to people who liked to write letters to *Playboy*.

Wilson and Shea did their best to make sense of what was going on. The modern conception of the 'conspiracy theory' was emerging, fully formed, just a few brief years after the flaws in the Warren Commission report into the JFK assassination had become evident. People were now openly accusing sections of the U.S. Government of being involved in Kennedy's death, an idea that would have been unthinkable to the average American when the murder occurred in 1963. To Wilson and Shea, as they waded through all the different accusations, it started to look like *everyone* had killed Kennedy. Some blamed the CIA, others the Mafia. Some claimed that it was Castro, while others pointed to anti-Castro forces. As they joked to each other, what if every conspiracy were true? From all this came the idea for the three-novel series that they wrote together between 1969 and 1971, the award winning *Illuminatus!* trilogy, which they dedicated to Hill and Thornley.

The wilfully complicated plot of the book essentially boils down to a struggle between order and chaos. It features a secret organization of enlightened beings called the Illuminati, who secretly rule the world for their own evil ends. The Illuminati was a real organisation that had been founded in 1776 in Bavaria with the aim of exploring and spreading Enlightenment ideals. Shea and Wilson claimed that the organisation has existed in secrecy ever since, and even for centuries before, although most historians believe that it only lasted for about ten years.

In the book, the Illuminati are opposed only by small groups of Discordians, who have to prevent the Illuminati from bringing about the end of the world. The Discordians, in true Discordian fashion, go under many names, such as the ELF (the Erisian

Liberation Front), the LDD (The League of Dynamic Discord, also known as Little Deluded Dopes) and The Justified Ancients of Mummu, otherwise known as the JAMs. The JAMs are "at least as old as the Illuminati and represent the primeval power of Chaos." They were once part of the Illuminati, but rebelled in order fight for chaos. As a side line, they had also set up a record company to create some decent music. The rest of the music industry was controlled by the Illuminati, the book explained, which was how they were able to incorporate the anti-JAMs slogan "Kick out the Jams, motherfuckers!" into MC5 records.

Needless to say, publishers were initially baffled by the whole thing. Eventually, after four years of effort, the first volume was published in 1975. It has remained in print ever since and gone on to win awards and inspire conspiracy fiction from *Foucault's Pendulum* to *The Da Vinci Code*, as well as countless video games and comic books. It planted the idea into modern culture that the Illuminati are an organisation who are currently active and who secretly run the world. This idea was intended as no more than a joke, or a 'mindfuck'. Nevertheless, there are now countless conspiracy theorists around the world who now believe it to be true. Imaginary ideas have a way of being just as influential, it seems, as more grounded ones.

## A Play on Illuminatus!

Ken Campbell was paying for a stack of books in Compendium, an independent esoteric bookshop in Camden, when he noticed a copy of *Illuminatus!* on display by the till. He was searching for some science fiction that might be suitable to adapt into his next project, because, following a pleasant evening drinking with the sci-fi author Brian Aldiss, he had decided that he quite liked the company of science fiction people. So it was that in 1976 Campbell and the writer and actor Chris Langham formed the Science Fiction Theatre of Liverpool, with the intention of creating a play to stage at Aunt Twackies. All he had to do now was find some science fiction.

His eye was drawn to this one book because it had a yellow submarine on the cover, an iconic image with obvious connections to Liverpool. The book itself is not science fiction, but booksellers had not known what to make of it and had placed it on the science fiction shelves for want of anywhere better. This, it seemed, was good enough for the Science Fiction Theatre of Liverpool.

Of all the books that he had bought, it was *Illuminatus!* that grabbed Campbell, in a way that none of the others did. Reading it was an eye-opener; it made him see the world differently. What had previously appeared to be hierarchical, ordered and neatly categorized now appeared as random connections of chance and ignorance. This effect was not just limited to the world in the book. The real world itself was changed, or at least how he perceived it. *Illuminatus!* made him simultaneously wiser and more baffled. It was good stuff.

Campbell decided to turn the entire trilogy into a cycle of five plays, lasting a total of eight and a half hours. There would be 23 actors playing over three hundred distinct parts. And this epic tale of global domination would be told on a small stage at the back of the warehouse café. Most people would not consider this to be a plausible goal, but Campbell just went ahead and did it anyway. As he saw it, things were only really worth doing if they were impossible. To quote the actor Chris Langham, who co-wrote the play with Campbell, "if it's possible it will end up as some mediocre, grant-subsidised bit of well-intentioned bourgeois bollocks. But if it's impossible, then it will assume an energy of its own, despite everything we do or don't do."

This was an attitude that Campbell drilled into Bill Drummond, whom he recruited to produce the sets for the show. It was never going to be easy. Campbell's key piece of direction to the cast and crew was, when thinking about the tone of what they were doing, to keep asking the question 'Is it heroic?' Drummond went back to the table in the back room that doubled as his workshop and painted the phrase 'Is it heroic?' on the wall in white paint. He then got to work.

As cast member Bill Nighy would later remember, "...and fuck me, did he deliver!" Drummond's solution was to build the sets to strange scales, utilizing tricks such as foreshortening and strange angles, all of which perfectly suited the disorienting style of the play. Tables or beds were stood upwards and stuck to the rear wall, giving the audience the impression that they were looking down on the action from the ceiling. Despite the seemingly contradictory scales of the story and the cafe stage, Drummond took Campbell's advice, assumed that the impossible would be possible, and just knuckled down and did it. And why not? Everyone was achieving things previously unimaginable. Jim Broadbent recalled the production of *Illuminatus!* working on a "genius level... It's wasn't that Ken was being a genius...it was the whole creation of doing the greatest show yet done on Planet World... his creative imagination was just stunning."

The success of the play led to a move south, and a sold-out run at the National Theatre in London began in March 1977. It now featured a pre-recorded prologue performed by John Gielgud, who played a computer called the First Universal Cybernetic Kinetic Ultramicro Programmer, or FUCKUP ("The best anarchist joke ever perpetrated at the heart of the National," in the view of Campbell's biographer Michael Coveney.) It also featured Robert Anton Wilson himself, who was given a role that involved lying naked on the stage shouting Aleister Crowley's maxim, "Do what thou will shall be the whole of the law!" Wilson also brought a large amount of acid with him, which he offered to the cast. Bill Nighy recalls that "everyone went very quiet and then... 'Yeah, why not, thanks,' and we all dived in. So we were all tripping. It's a terrible idea if you want to act, but there you are..."

For many in the audience for the National Theatre run, this was their first exposure to Discordian ideas. Among them was young artist Jimmy Cauty. Cauty, then aged 22, had already had some success painting best-selling *Lord of the Rings* and *The Hobbit* posters for Athena (they were bought, he said, "mainly by student nurses".) He did not, however, meet Bill Drummond at this performance. Drummond had disappeared from the project back in Liverpool. After the sets were completed and as the premiere of the play grew nearer, Drummond had announced that he was just popping out to get some glue…and never returned. It was the late Seventies and punk was starting to rumble. As radical as the book and play were, the spirit of the age was not emerging in the form of eight and a half hour plays. Together with Ian Broudie, then a young guitarist whom Campbell had recruited to perform music for the play, Drummond formed the band *Big In Japan*.

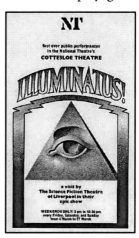

Poster for National Theatre presentation of *Illuminatus!*

Campbell had shown Drummond that the impossible was only impossible if you did not stand up and do it. It did not matter how big the practical problems were, or how crazy the enterprise may seem. Drummond took that attitude, got a bass guitar, and went off to make music. Years later, on New Year's Day 1987, he would phone Jimmy Cauty (whom he finally met whilst working in A&R for Warners) and suggest that the pair form a band called The Justified Ancients of Mu Mu. Under that name (and also as The KLF, a name they would increasingly use as their career progressed) they would bring the Discordian spirit of chaos to the music industry.

## Full of Sheet 8

Anyone who has been in a position which involves reading record company press releases will know that they contain more unreadable bullshit than any other literary medium. An awkward amalgam of romantic fawning and angry political manifestos, music industry releases are frequently a stream-of-consciousness outpouring of rare and unlikely superlatives, written by people without first-hand knowledge of the music they refer to. The releases issued by Drummond and Cauty do not, at first glance, appear to be much different.

The statement issued in February 1990 and titled "Information Sheet 8" is a typical example. It begins with a classic summation of their debt to Robert Anton Wilson: "THE JUSTIFIED ANCIENTS OF MUMU are an organization (or disorganization) who are at least as old as the ILLUMINATI. They represent the primeval power of Chaos. As such they are diametrically opposed to the order that the Illuminati try to oppress on mankind and on mankind's understanding of the Universe."

It goes on to explain how Drummond and Cauty took on that mantle in order to make records without "anyone telling them how it should be done." But within days of their first record being released, the statement continues…

> …they began to receive mail and messages from very strange sources. The information they were getting was varied and confusing. They were being warned not to get involved with what they could never understand. They were being threatened. They were being congratulated in taking The War above ground. They were being welcomed on board as 'brothers in arms' in the only war that was ever justified, I quote; 'To finally separate Time from Space, thus enabling Chaos once again to reign supreme.'

Most readers of music press releases would have skipped all this, under the assumption that it was bullshit. To anyone familiar with Operation Mindfuck, however, it seems extremely familiar. This raises the question as to whether Discordians were still engaging in those tactics in the 1980s, and directing them at Cauty and Drummond.

There is actually good evidence that Discordians did target the pair with hoax letters. In Pete Robinson's well regarded JAMs history/fanzine *Justified And Ancient History*, he records a 1987 letter from an American called 'Don Lucknowe' who threatened them with 'Deep Shit' if they continued using that name. Drummond and Cauty were worried that they faced legal action from Wilson and they did not reply to the letter because, according to Robinson, they were "shit scared."

Robinson did make contact on their behalf, however. The address was for a now-defunct parody news magazine called *Yossarian Universal*. The editor, Paul Fericano, replied to Robinson and told him that they believed that *Yossarian Universal* contributing editor James Wallis was responsible for the original letter. Wallis was a big Three Stooges fan, and the name 'Don Lucknowe' is based on a Stooges' catchphrase 'Don't Look Now.'" This interest in Three Stooges-style comedy was a typical Discordian touch (Discordians are the type of people who consider Harpo Marx's birthday a Holy day, after all.) According to Fericano, Wallis was "somewhat of a hoaxer, in our *YU* tradition (it's one of our trademarks – and that's an understatement.)"

Assigning any particular hoax letter to Operation Mindfuck is by definition extremely difficult. Wilson and Shea have explained that no Discordian...

> ...knows for sure who is or who is not involved in any phase of Operation Mindfuck or what activities they are or are not engaged in as part of that project. Thus, the outsider is immediately trapped in a double-bind: the only safe assumption is that anything a Discordian does is somehow related to Operation Mindfuck, but, since this leads directly to paranoia, this is not a 'safe' assumption after all, and the 'risky' hypothesis that whatever the Discordians are doing is harmless may be 'safer' in the long run.

There is a good reason to consider *Yossarian Universal*'s letter to The JAMs to be part of the Operation Mindfuck, however. 'Yossarian' is the protagonist in Joseph Heller's *Catch 22* and is also, according to *Illuminatus!*, a Discordian Saint.

Fericano's letter ends, "Sorry if all this caused anxiety, etc. Tell the members of the KLF that I wish them well, and would love to hear their music. Have never been able to find [music by The JAMs] out here." All this seems highly plausible. The British music press was widely available in the US, and a story about how ABBA's lawyers demanded the destruction of albums by The Justified Ancients of Mu Mu due to copyright issues was widely reported. The records themselves, however, did not cross the Atlantic in any numbers (indeed, most copies of their debut album were burnt in a field in Sweden). All that American Discordians knew about The JAMs would have been what they saw in the press, and all the adverts that Drummond and Cauty placed in the music press included a P.O. Box address. It seems likely, then, that American Discordians began sending strange and bewildering letters to Cauty and Drummond, believing that their adoption of the name 'Justified Ancients of Mu Mu' made them clear and deserving targets for Operation Mindfuck.

With that in mind, a further claim in Information Sheet 8 is worth noting. Drummond and Cauty claimed that their solicitor was sent...

> ...a contract with an organization or individual calling themselves 'Eternity'. The wording of this contract was that of standard music business legal speak, but the terms discussed and the rights required and granted were of a far stranger kind.

"Whether The Contract was a very clever and intricate prank by a legal minded JAMS fan was of little concern to Drummond and Cauty," Information Sheet 8 continues….

For them it was as good a marker as anything as to what direction their free style career should take next.... In the first term of The Contract they, Drummond and Cauty, were required to make an artistic representation of themselves on a journey to a place called THE WHITE ROOM. The medium they chose to make this representation was up to them. Where or what THE WHITE ROOM was, was never clearly defined. Interpretation was left to their own creativity. The remuneration they are to receive on completion of this work of art was supposed to be access to THE "real" WHITE ROOM.

The pair claim that they went on to sign this contract, despite the advice of their solicitor to have nothing to do with it. It is worth noting at this juncture that Cauty and Drummond were ignorant of Operation Mindfuck. Their sole knowledge of Discordianism came from *Illuminatus!*, which Cauty had never read and which Drummond had not, at that time, ever finished. By signing any such contract they were not simply 'playing along', for they would have had no context for what the contract was, or where it had come from.

In this reading of events, Drummond and Cauty appear to have taken a Discordian Operation Mindfuck prank letter at face value, and spent hundreds of thousands of pounds making a piece of work that would fulfil their part of a hoax contract that they chose to sign.

As to what the 'real' White Room which the contract alluded to was, Drummond and Cauty were typically candid: "Your guess is as good as anybody's." In Discordian terms, however, the meaning is relatively clear. The White Room refers to illumination, or enlightenment. The word 'room,' however, is interesting. The use of a spatial metaphor defines enlightenment as a place that can be travelled to, or sought in a quest. The search for the White Room becomes a pilgrimage, with the White Room itself taking on the character of the Holy Grail. Drummond and Cauty's film, when seen in this light, becomes a means to an end. *The White Room* was not intended as a film that would make money or enhance their careers. It was, instead, a step along the path in a search for enlightenment.

## Discord in The White Room

The first hint that the film was not going to be released came in an information sheet from December 1989. "As you may already know the film was finished this summer and release was planned for autumn," it said. "However, some strange things have happened to the KLF and they have decided to dramatically re-enact these events for inclusion in the film. For this further filming they need to lay their hands on a million pounds."

The story goes that, following a gig at Heaven, they were accosted by a homeless guy called Mickey McElwee who told them the following tale: Before his life fell apart, McElwee used to do occasional jobs for an international arms dealer called Silverman. Silverman recruited McElwee to follow Drummond and Cauty to Spain during the filming of *The White Room*, in order to observe them at a distance. Silverman believed that Drummond and Cauty had been contacted by the actual Justified Ancients of Mummu, a secret organisation who not only existed but whose intention was to bring about nuclear war for shits and giggles. As McElwee watched the filming from a distance, he realised that a third party was also watching. This person, who McElwee believed was working for the British Government and who also knew of the existence of the 'real' Justified Ancients of Mu Mu, was intending to assassinate Drummond and Cauty with a sniper's rifle. Drummond was apparently nearly shot during the filming of a scene where he walks up to a large Spanish castle. His life was saved, or the so the story went, because McElwee killed the assassin before he could fire.

When Drummond and Cauty retold this story, they stressed that McElwee was probably a deranged fan who had made the whole thing up but, nevertheless, the incident had scared the living crap out of them.

A more cynical interpretation, such as the one held by this author, is that they made this part of the story up. The 'ambient road movie' version of *The White Room*, it was acknowledged, was largely perceived as being very boring. It was hard to see why any viewer would care about the two directionless seekers on screen. Weaving a conspiracy-based version of the JAMs mythology into things, however, allowed them to keep the expensive footage that they had already shot and, at the same time, deliver a more traditional conspiracy thriller about two men who had become way out of their depth.

There were a few problems with this approach, however. The first is that all the Discordian humour had somehow become lost in translation, resulting in the fatal mistake of taking the whole thing seriously. The moment it is supposed that The Justified Ancients of Mummu is a real secret organisation that actually exists, then all that is interesting about them evaporates. In a related problem, the script for this version of the film was terrible. It would have resulted in something far worse than what they already had. The ambient road movie version may have been considered too boring to many to sit through, but it did at least succeed on its own terms.

Nevertheless the new script, which now included a dramatic recreation of McElwee's story intercut with the existing footage, was budgeted. Paul McGann, who would later become the eighth Doctor Who, was cast in the role of McElwee. All that they had to do was raise the extra million pounds that filming this new script would entail.

To do this, they attempted to recreate the success of "Doctorin' The TARDIS" and produce another number one record. Cauty and Drummond entered the studio and emerged with a cheesy pop single called "Kylie Said To Jason". This, however, failed to even enter the top 100. Without the money they expected "Kylie Said To Jason" to make, they had no way of funding the rest of the film.

The soundtrack album for *The White Room* finally emerged in 1991. It was a critical and commercial hit which is still found in many '100 Best Albums' lists to this day. Drummond and Cauty successfully rode the spirit of Discord right into the heart of the music industry, igniting a chain of events that would eventually lead to them literally burning a million pounds in cash in a boathouse on the isle of Jura.

The film, however, was dead. The existing version was never released, and the final script was never shot. The 'real' White Room, of course, was never found. As Drummond once remarked, "[completing] that road movie thing, it can only end in death. We're not ready for that yet."

**J.M.R. Higgs** is a writer and director from Brighton, England. He is the author of *The Brandy of the Damned* and *I Have America Surrounded: The Life of Timothy Leary*, and he blogs at www.jmrhiggs.com.

# Origin of the Space Gods

### Ancient Astronauts and the Cthulhu Mythos in Fiction and Fact

by *Jason Colavito*

One of the most dramatic ideas found in H. P. Lovecraft's weird fiction known as the Cthulhu Mythos is the suggestion that extraterrestrial beings arrived on earth in the distant past, were responsible for ancient works of monumental stone architecture, and inspired mankind's earliest mythologies and religions. In the 1970s, this basic premise was resurrected as the "ancient astronaut theory," a fringe hypothesis that gained widespread popularity thanks to Swiss hotelier Erich von Däniken's book *Chariots of the Gods?* (1968) and its television adaptation, *In Search of Ancient Astronauts* (1973), hosted by Rod Serling, of *Twilight Zone* fame. According to research done by Kenneth L. Feder, at the height of von Däniken's popularity in the

1970s and '80s one in four college students accepted the ancient astronaut theory, but twenty years later less than ten percent did.[1]

Though mainstream science does not recognize extraterrestrial intervention in human history, the theory continues to receive exposure on cable television documentaries, in magazines, and in a plethora of books.

Providence, Rhode Island author H.P. Lovecraft (1890-1937) has been justly hailed as a master of the horror story, and his work claims a place beside Edgar Allan Poe and Stephen King in the pantheon of the genre. Born into a wealthy family in 1890, Lovecraft's life was a series of reverses and declines as his family lost their fortune and his parents succumbed to madness. He was a precocious and self-taught scholar who read voraciously and devoured as much literature as he could read. He read the novels of H.G.Wells, whose *War of the Worlds* told of the coming of alien creatures to earth. He also read the eighteenth-century Gothic masters of horror, and above all Edgar Allan Poe. He also read works of pseudoscience and mysticism for inspiration.

When he set about writing his own works, he began to blend the modern world of science fiction with his favorite tales of Gothic gloom. Lovecraft tried to bring the Gothic tale into the twentieth century, modernizing the trappings of ancient horror for a new century of science. Lovecraft published his work in pulp fiction magazines, notably *Weird Tales*, though some of his works were not published until after his death in 1937. Throughout the 1940s and 1950s, science fiction and horror magazines reprinted Lovecraft's tales numerous times, and he became one of the most popular pulp authors.

Lovecraft's works banished the supernatural by recasting it in materialist terms. He took the idea of a pantheon of ancient gods and made them a group of aliens who descended to earth in the distant past.

Across his works, Lovecraft provided a number of different explanations for the arrival ancient visitors on the primeval earth. In

"The Call of Cthulhu," the Old Ones, including the tentacled, starborn Cthulhu, are said to have come "to the young world out of the sky" and to have raised mighty cities whose remains could be seen in the cyclopean stones dotting Pacific islands. These Old Ones brought with them images of themselves (thus inventing art) and hieroglyphs once legible but now unknown (the origins of writing). They spoke to humans in their dreams, and established a cult to worship them (the origins of religion). They appeared as, and were treated like, monstrous living gods, so great were their mystical powers:

> Old Castro remembered bits of hideous legend that paled the speculations of theosophists and made man and the world seem recent and transient indeed. There had been aeons when other Things ruled on the earth, and They had had great cities. Remains of Them, he said the deathless Chinamen had told him, were still be found as Cyclopean stones on islands in the Pacific. They all died vast epochs of time before men came, but there were arts which could revive Them when the stars had come round again to the right positions in the cycle of eternity. They had, indeed, come themselves from the stars, and brought Their images with Them. These Great Old Ones, Castro continued, were not composed altogether of flesh and blood. They had shape—for did not this star-fashioned image prove it?—but that shape was not made of matter. When the stars were right, They could plunge from world to world through the sky; but when the stars were wrong, They could not live.[2]

In later stories, Lovecraft added new details and altered his previous conception of the Old Ones to provide a richer and more developed picture of alien intervention in earth life. In *At the Mountains of Madness*, Lovecraft presents his most complete vision of the extraterrestrial origins of human life. Here, the Old Ones were now a separate species of alien creature at war with Great Cthulhu and his spawn, who only

'Yog-Sothoth', by Dominique Signoret (CCASA Licence)

arrived eons later. The Old Ones were "the originals of the fiendish elder myths" of ancient mythology,[3] and they raised great cities under the oceans and on the primitive continents. These beings arrived on earth after colonizing other planets, and they created life on earth as a source of food. These artificial primitive cells they allowed to evolve naturally into the plants and animals of the modern world—including primitive humanity, which they used as food or entertainment.

Elsewhere, Lovecraft described his ancient visitors as maintaining a presence on the modern earth, and like the Nephilim of the Bible, they begat children with earth women in "The Dunwich Horror," "The Shadow Over Innsmouth," and "Medusa's Coil." In "The Horror in the Museum," it is suggested that the monstrous creatures once worshipped as gods were not all extraterrestrials, and that some may have come from alternate dimensions. In *The Shadow Out of Time*, the extraterrestrial Great Race is one of countless species spanning the universe, and their mental powers let them project themselves backward and forward in time, gathering intelligence and knowledge for their library and, in places, imparting their own wisdom. Most to the point, in his ghostwriting of William Lumley's "The Diary of Alonzo Typer" the title narrator learns from the pre-human *Book of Dzyan* that aliens from Venus came to earth in spaceships to "civilize" the planet.

Human knowledge of these aliens is fragmentary and obscure. Evidence exists in the form of anomalous ancient artifacts of pre-human manufacture, garbled folklore and mythology, and written texts like the *Necronomicon, Nameless Cults,* and the *Book of Eibon,* which hint at but do not fully disclose the extraterrestrials' nature and habits.

Many critics of Lovecraft have noted that his vision for the Mythos changed over time, as the godlike and semi-supernatural Cthulhu of "The Call of Cthulhu" gradually gave way to the fully material aliens of *At the Mountains of Madness;* in time faux mythology gave way to faux science in the Mythos. Many Mythos writers, beginning with August Derleth, were dismayed by the contradictions in Lovecraft's writing (e.g., Cthulhu is an Old One in "Cthulhu" but merely their "cousin" in "The Dunwich Horror"; the Old Ones change identity several times, too), and they have attempted to systematize the Mythos. However, Lovecraft's writings reflect the way real myths develop, with changes and contradictions and anomalies. This is compounded by the fact that Lovecraft did not write as an omniscient narrator but rather presented his Mythos through the eyes of scholars and writers who had only part of the story and therefore could not offer the whole truth. Even in the *Necronomicon* Abdul Alhazred (it is implied) was privy only to hints and rumors and interpreted the Mythos through the guise of the Near Eastern mythologies he knew. "These viscous masses were without doubt what Abdul Alhazred whispered about as the 'Shoggoths' in his frightful *Necronomicon*, though even that mad Arab had not hinted that any existed on earth except in the dreams of those who had chewed a certain alkaloidal herb."[4]

In other words, Lovecraft's Mythos tales show us a fragmented, shifting, and uncertain view of the alien beings reflected through the biases and prejudices and mental limits of those who encounter them.

## Ancient Astronauts before Lovecraft

The idea that life could exist on other worlds was not unique to Lovecraft, of course, and the concept had a long history dating back to early Greek philosophers who speculated on the nature of beings on other worlds. Anaxagoras (c. 500-428 BCE) proposed that life began from "seeds" that littered the universe; Anaxarchus (c. 340 BCE) thought there to be an infinity of worlds, and Epicurus (c. 341-270 BCE) felt life existed on many planets across the vastness of space. These philosophers, though, did not propose the visitation of these aliens to the earth.

The most important early writer to propose extraterrestrial visitation on earth was Madame Helena Blavatsky (1831-1891), the founder of Theosophy, a Victorian-era amalgam of Spiritualism, Eastern religions, and good old-fashioned hokum. In *The Secret Doctrine*, Theosophy's most important text, Blavatsky noted Greek speculation about life on other worlds and asserted that the ancients had first-hand knowledge of the fact of extraterrestrial existence. She speculated that the beings on the innumerable inhabited worlds may have "influence" or "control" over the earth. She also asserted that spiritual beings originating on the moon contributed to the metaphysical development of earth life:

> The first race of men were, then, simply the images, the astral doubles, of their Fathers, who were the pioneers, or the most progressed Entities from a preceding though *lower* sphere, the shell of which is now our Moon. But even this shell is all-potential, for, having generated the Earth, it is the *phantom* of the Moon which, attracted by magnetic affinity, sought to form its first inhabitants, the pre-human monsters.[5]

But for her any alien intervention is a sideline to the epic history of evolutionary and spiritual developments of an assortment of earth creatures who grew from primal ooze to Aryan supremacy on the lost continents of Hyperborea, Lemuria, and Atlantis.

Blavatsky's disciple W. Scott-Elliot expanded on hints in the Theosophical cosmos by creating a race of divine beings inhabiting Venus. In *The Lost Lemuria* (1904), Scott-Elliot claimed that beings that evolved on Venus but had reached a spiritual or "divine" stage of development came to earth and taught the inhabitants of Lemuria the arts of civilization and gave them wheat and fire.[6] A critical difference between the Lords of Venus, Blavatsky's moon creatures, and Mythos beings (and indeed modern ancient astronauts) is that the Theosophical Venusians and lunarians are not envisioned as true extraterrestrials (in the modern sense) from distant star systems but as incarnations of spiritual beings who share a mystic connection to earth creatures and feel a spiritual calling to aid their brethren on earth. Here, the Venusians are inhabitants of Venus in the same sense that the angels of God were once thought to inhabit Venus, Mars, and the other crystalline spheres that surrounded the earth. As Scott-Eliot put it:

> The positions occupied by the divine beings from the Venus chain were naturally those of rulers, instructors in religion, and teachers of the arts, and it is in this latter capacity that a reference to the arts taught by them comes to our aid in the consideration of the history of this early race, continued.[7]

In 1919, the great collector of anomalous trivia, Charles Fort, published *The Book of the Damned*, in which he speculated that old stories of demons could be related to "undesirable visitors from other worlds,"[8] though he did not draw a firm connection between devils and aliens. He also suggested that other worlds may have communicated with ours in the distant past, left behind advanced technology, or attempted to colonize the earth.[9] "If other worlds have ever in the past had relations with this earth, they were attempted positivizations: to extend themselves, by colonies, upon this earth; to convert, or assimilate, indigenous inhabitants of this earth."[10]

However, Fort made no claim that such things actually happened, only that they *may* have happened, and at any rate there is no way to tell whether the creatures were alien, trans-dimensional, spiritual, or even imaginary—perhaps the result of telepathy, communications from the spirit realm, or from myriad other sources.

H. P. Lovecraft read both *The Book of the Damned* and Scott-Eliot's compilation volume *The Story of Atlantis and Lost Lemuria* (1925), and from these fragmentary ideas about prehistoric extraterrestrial visitation imagined (more-or-less) flesh-and-blood aliens arriving on earth in the distant past and all that this implied.

## ANCIENT ASTRONAUTS AFTER LOVECRAFT

Lovecraft's Mythos became one of the touchstones of modern horror literature and a powerful theme in horror, fantasy, and science fiction, where the idea of alien visitors in the deep past continues to enjoy popularity in contemporary works like *Stargate, The X-Files, Doctor Who, Alien vs. Predator*, and hundreds of other movies, books, and television shows. However, Lovecraft's alien gods also spawned the decidedly non-fiction (if not factual) ancient astronaut theory, which continues to convert new adherents today.

The names of Lovecraft's alien gods, like Cthulhu, Yog-Sothoth, and Shub-Niggurath, began to crop up in other stories during Lovecraft's lifetime. Lovecraft himself started this practice by inserting these names, or variants on them, into stories he ghostwrote or revised for other authors. In his revision of Zelia Bishop's "The Mound," for example, Lovecraft slipped his alien god Cthulhu into the story under the variant name Tulu, giving magazine readers what they thought were independent stories featuring references to the same ancient gods. By the 1960s, several dozen authors were using elements of what came to be called "The Cthulhu Mythos" in stories they wrote for science fiction and horror magazines.

Lovecraftian fiction became increasingly popular in Europe, where the French embraced him as a bent genius, much as they embraced Edgar Allan Poe. In France, the Russian expatriate Jacques Bergier and the writer Louis Pauwels read Lovecraft and were inspired by his cosmic vision. Bergier claimed to have corresponded with Lovecraft in 1935, though no letters survive. He spent much of the 1950s promoting Lovecraft in the French media, including the magazine he and Pauwels edited, *Planète*, and working to bring Lovecraft's work out in French editions. The *Planète's* editors held Lovecraft as their prophet, and their reprints of his stories helped to popularize him and the Cthulhu Mythos in the French imagination.

Digging into Lovecraft's Theosophical and Fortean source material, Bergier and Pauwels wrote *Le Matin des magiciens* (1960) (published in English as *The Morning of the Magicians*) and presented the first fully-fledged modern ancient astronaut theory. In it, they presented the themes found in Lovecraft as non-fiction, speculating about such alternative history touchstones as the "true" origin of the Egyptian pyramids, ancient maps that appear to have been drawn from outer space, advanced technology incongruously placed in the ancient past, and the other staples of later ancient astronaut theories. They note that ancient mythologies are replete with gods who visit earth in fiery chariots and return to the sky. These, they state, may have been alien visitors in spaceships.

The Sphinx and Pyramids of Giza, frequently claimed evidence of alien visitation.
(Library of Congress)

Pauwels and Bergier drew on unrelated writings from a number of French and other authors who wondered to a greater or lesser extent that modern UFO sightings might have antecedents in prehistory, but they combined this 1950s space-age speculation with a Lovecraftian cosmic vision and a New Age sensibility that translated Cthulhu into an ancient astronaut in a way that shiny atom-age extraterrestrials in spacesuits never could.

*Morning of the Magicians* became one of the most important sources for Erich von Däniken, the Swiss writer whose *Chariots of the Gods?* (1968) brought what had hitherto been a theory known only to Theosophists, Lovecraft aficionados, and fringe theorists into the cultural mainstream. Von Däniken did not mention Pauwels and Bergier in his works, however, until a potential lawsuit forced him to disclose the sources he closely paraphrased in *Chariots*. The bibliography of *Chariots* thereafter listed the French writers' book in its 1962 German translation, *Aufbruch ins dritte Jahrtausend*. Tens of millions of copies of *Chariots* and its sequels sold, and the ancient astronaut theory became a cultural phenomenon, appearing in movies, on Johnny Carson's *Tonight Show*, in *Playboy*, and practically anywhere people were talking about the past.

Other authors were inspired by von Däniken's theories, including Robert Temple (whose *The Sirius Mystery* argued that amphibious aliens from Sirius taught Sumerians civilization) and Zecharia Sitchin (whose *The Twelfth Planet* argued that aliens from a "wandering" planet called Nibiru conquered ancient earth to steal its gold and other precious metals). By the end of the 1970s, there was an entire network of authors and promoters then known as the Ancient Astronaut Society (later the Archaeology, Astronautics and SETI Research Association, or AAS RA). As of this writing, the H2 channel broadcasts *Ancient Aliens: The Series*, a weekly program that explores the work of von Däniken and other ancient astronaut theorists. The program was seen by more than two million viewers each week when it aired on the History Channel before it moved to sister station H2 in 2012. The ancient astronaut theory also appeared in movies and television series, ranging from the various incarnations of *Stargate* to Ridley Scott's *Prometheus* (2012), a film that the famed *Alien* director explicitly modeled on von Däniken's 1970s bestsellers:

> NASA and the Vatican agree that is almost mathematically impossible that we can be where we are today without there being a little help along the way… That's what we're looking at (in the film), at some of Eric von Daniken's ideas of how did we humans come about.[11]

So what made so many believe aliens visited our ancestors?

## The Evidence for Aliens

The ancient astronaut theory, as it developed in the hands of Pauwels and Bergier, von Däniken, and others, uses a combination of suggestive archaeological, mythological, and artistic evidence. Though believers interpret nearly every piece of ancient history as supporting the ancient astronaut theory, in outline, the most important evidence is as follows:

*Archaeological*

Believers maintain that ancient cities and monuments the world over display three important properties that speak to their non-human origins. First, many are composed of stones that weigh so much that it seems impossible for ordinary humans to have moved them. For example, the blocks making up the Great Pyramid of Egypt weigh as much as fifty tons each, and the stones of the Incan fortress of Sacsayhuaman weigh as much as two hundred tons. Further, believers hold that these ancient sites are laid out and constructed

Inca masonry, which ancient astronaut theorists believe is too perfect to be the sole work of human beings. (Library of Congress)

with a precision that is unmatched by all but the most modern of contemporary constructions. The Great Pyramid, for instance, is said to be placed on a base within 0.049 inches of flat; its sides are oriented to the cardinal directions within three minutes of arc, something unmatched in nearly all modern constructions. Such engineering is said to be possible only with alien help, either as the builders themselves or as teachers who imparted the knowledge of such building techniques.

Second, believers argue that ancient sites and artifacts encode scientific data that should be unknown to Stone Age peoples. The Great Pyramid, to take a familiar example, is said to be an accurate scale model of the northern hemisphere of the earth thousands of years before Eratosthenes first estimated the planet's circumference. It is also said to be placed in the exact center of the earth's land masses. The monumental pyramids of the ancient Mexican city of Teotihuacan are often said to be a scale model of the solar system.

Third, anomalous artifacts represent advanced technology of possibly inhuman origin. The famous "Baghdad battery" is a small jar that may have held electrodes that when exposed to vinegar could have produced a small electrical charge. Small golden bees from Mexico may be depictions of ancient airplanes. A sparkplug may have been found inside a billion-year-old rock known as the Coso artifact.

*Mythological*

Ancient myths and legends record the arrival of the aliens and their deeds upon the earth. Believers in the ancient astronaut theory are united in their belief that myths and holy books are factual accounts of events that happened in the real world. The apocryphal Book of Enoch is a favorite, along with the legend of the Jewish prophet ascending to heaven in a fiery chariot. The Biblical vision of Ezekiel, who saw a fiery apparition of interlocking wheels, is said to represent an encounter with a flying saucer. The destruction of Sodom and

*Jason Returns with the Golden Fleece* by Ugo da Carpi, c. 1500. Von Däniken believes Greek gods were aliens, the Golden Fleece was really an alien helicopter, and Jason's ship, the Argo, was really an alien spacecraft. (Library of Congress)

Gomorrah in fire and brimstone is suggested to be an account of aliens dropping an atomic bomb. Elsewhere, mythological appearances of savior gods such as Oannes in Sumer, Osiris in Egypt, Quetzalcoatl in Mexico, and Viracocha in Peru are thought to be factual accounts of anthropomorphic aliens bringing civilization to benighted ancient tribes. Hindu mythology is an especially rich source of proof because of its descriptions of flying machines, ray guns, and explosions that resemble atomic detonations.

And of course, like the Old Ones in *At the Mountains of Madness*, the gods who created humans and other earth life in myth and religion are here interpreted as aliens that genetically engineered earth life for their inscrutable purposes. They also manage earth life, like the Old Ones who wipe out unfavorable races, by sending floods or annihilating trouble spots with nuclear weapons.

*Artistic*

Ancient art shows images of the aliens and their advanced technology, according to believers. Aboriginal cave art in Australia depicts beings with circles around their heads, obviously the helmets of space-faring aliens. Similarly, ancient Japanese statuary of rotund monsters actually shows aliens in bulky spacesuits. Medieval paintings are said to contain images of flying discs or aerodynamic chariots that resemble flying saucers and rocket ships. The lid of the tomb of the Mayan king Pacal at Palenque does not show the king in the underworld but rather depicts him at the controls of technological device, perhaps a rocket ship. An image of a lotus blossom in the Egyptian temple of Dendera is really a depiction of a light bulb, complete with power cord and filament. Ancient maps are believed to show a) earth as depicted from space, b) the world as it existed in the Ice Age before human civilization, c) Antarctica centuries before its discovery in 1818.

## The Science

Archaeologists, paleontologists, anthropologists, and other scientific professionals were less than impressed by the web of suggestion and interpretation that masqueraded as a scientific hypothesis. Since the mid-1970s, skeptics have produced articles, books, and documentaries aimed at debunking the ancient astronaut theory and explaining its "evidence" as a series of misinterpretations, misrepresentations, and ignorance of scientific research. It would be impossible to thoroughly explore the scientific arguments against the ancient astronaut theory in anything short of a book (for which, see my 2005 book, the *The Cult of Alien Gods*[12]), but the general lines of argument run like this:

*Archaeological*

No evidence of extraterrestrial technology has ever been found on earth, and no artifact can conclusively be tied to a planet other than earth. Such claims are exaggerations, misinterpretations, or frauds. For example, the alleged Coso artifact is not a billion-year-old bit of advanced technology but a 1920s spark plug encrusted in solidified crud mistaken for ancient rock. Ancient monuments show every sign of being constructed by the ancient people who lived around them, as demonstrated by the artifacts found in, around, on top of, and under ancient sites. Construction of buildings—even highly precise and heavy ones—can be accomplished with large numbers of people working together.

*Mythological*

Ancient myths do not have a direct correlation with events in the distant past. Instead, they are complex web of symbolism, religious belief, historical events, and imagination. There may be some

Stonehenge. Despite centuries of investigation, no alien artifacts have ever been found in, around, or under Stonehenge. (Library of Congress)

distorted truth behind myths (as the discovery of Troy proved for Homer's *Iliad*), but they cannot be interpreted as literal accounts of historic happenings. Nor are the myths themselves consistent across time. The myth of Jason and the Golden Fleece, for example, shows significant changes to major events between its earliest recorded forms and the best-known version, written by Apollonius of Rhodes many centuries later. In the earliest forms of the myth, it is unclear whether the Golden Fleece was even present—a far cry from those like Robert Temple or Erich von Däniken who assumed that one version of the myth stood for all, could be considered definitive, and could be interpreted literally as evidence of alien intervention. Mythology must be seen in its cultural context, and any interpretation must account for changes, distortions, and mutations that accrue over time as oral stories are retold, come into contact with stories from other cultures and lands, and eventually take on a written form. This is not unlike the contradictory variants of Mythos legends found in Lovecraft's own stories.

*Artistic*

Again, ancient art should not be taken as a literal recording of events happening before the artists' eyes. Many works of prehistoric art, such as cave paintings, depict shamans engaged in rituals designed to imbue them with the powers of the netherworld and their spirit animals. These cannot be taken literally but must be seen in cultural context and in terms of the visions of strange shapes and forms humans see when in shamanic trance states. Other pieces of ancient art, like the Dendera light bulb or Pacal's coffin lid, must be viewed in light of other artistic depictions from the period, not by itself, in order to understand the symbolism and artistic conventions used in the work. Neither seems so much like ancient depictions of technology when compared to other Egyptian depictions of the lotus, or Mayan funerary art. No one piece exists in isolation, and an interpretation based only on what something "looks like" instead of its place in the broader cultural picture will lead to mistaken correlations.

## Conclusions

The novelist and Lovecraft scholar Richard L. Tierney noted the potential correlations between Lovecraft's story "The Mound" (with Zealia Bishop) and actual Mesoamerican and Native American legends and traditions, and he identifies Yig, father of serpents, with the Aztec god Quetzalcoatl, the feathered serpent. At Teotihuacan, the Mexican city so old and mysterious that even the Aztecs themselves knew it only as a ruin belonging to the gods who descended from the sky, Tierney humorously identifies the sculptures of tentacled Tlaloc the rain god and serpentine Quetzalcoatl on Quetzalcoatl's temple as representations of Cthulhu and Yig.[13] Thus is the ancient astronaut theorists' evidence for aliens transformed again into proof of the Mythos. This, of course, was meant in jest, but the same reasoning transformed ancient achievements into alien interventions.

In 1982, Charles Garofalo and Robert M. Price wrote an article for *Crypt of Cthulhu* noting the similarities between the Mythos and Erich von Däniken's ancient astronaut theories. They concluded that despite the high degree of correlation between von Däniken's evidence and claims and Lovecraft's fictional conceits, direct influence was impossible because von Däniken denied ever having read or heard of Lovecraft.[14] As we have seen, though, the influence need not be direct. The connections between those who propose ancient astronauts as fact and those who write of them as (science) fiction are myriad, and the web of influence runs in many directions. Perhaps someday the Great Race will swap minds with some of us and tell the world how aliens once ruled the past, but until that happens, Cthulhu will have to rest in his tomb and the ancient astronauts will have to stay in their fictional chariots.

**Jason Colavito** is an author and editor in Albany, NY whose work explores the connections between science, pseudoscience, and speculative fiction. His investigations examine the way human beings create and employ the supernatural to alter and understand our reality and our world. His books include *The Cult of Alien Gods: H.P. Lovecraft and Extraterrestrial Pop Culture* (Prometheus Books, 2005) and his most recent, *Cthulhu in World Mythology* (Atomic Overmind, 2012). He writes frequently about the weird and the wild at JasonColavito.com.

# House of the Swastika

### Hermann Göring, the Edelweiss Society, and the Strange Connection to a Free Energy Pioneer

by *Theo Paijmans*

This night the old Norse gods rode out. Fierce snowstorms raged through the dark. In the skies between Stockholm and Rockelstad Castle, a single plane plowed stubbornly forward. The drone of the engine was hardly noticeable in the howling wind. The German pilot had seen worse, flying his Fokker plane on reconnaissance, bombing and attack missions over the trenches of World War One. It was 21 February 1920 though, and return to civilian life had been unbearable for the highly decorated flying ace with 22 confirmed victories. Having moved to Sweden, he had joined a civilian airline company. Now the former fighter ace and last commander of Manfred 'The Red Baron' von Richthofen's famous Flying Circus was for hire for private flights.

Struggling to pilot his plane through the stygian darkness on this stormy night was the result of such an assignment.

The passenger was no ordinary man either. The wealthy explorer and ethnographer[1] had requested the flight in order to return to the castle that was his. At his estate a huge bear – which he had taken with him as a cub on one of his many travels[2] – roamed freely. He was a pioneer in early Swedish aeronautics after his crossing of the Baltic Sea during the Finnish War of Freedom in 1918.[3] That year he had helped in founding the Finnish air force by donating its first plane. But tonight, his presence was urgently required at Rockelstad Castle. All train fares had been cancelled due to the weather conditions, so he had gone to the small airfield in Stockholm. Not one Swedish pilot was willing to fly through the snowstorm in the inky darkness, but the former German fighter-pilot had accepted.[4]

Struggling through the night with almost no visibility and no land beacons in sight, the pilot used the railway as guidance by following it at a low altitude. Having reached Sparreholm, the pilot turned south across the lake and landed on the ice below Rockelstad Castle. Freezing, they tied the plane to the steamboat jetty. As the dismal weather conditions made further flying impossible, the passenger offered the hospitality of his castle to the pilot. Fate had brought these two unlikely men together. The name of the pilot was Hermann Göring. The name of the passenger was Carl Gustaf Bloomfield Eric von Rosen, better known simply as Count Eric von Rosen.

## Rockelstad's Strange Legends

As with any ancient edifice, eerie stories swirled around Rockelstad Castle. In Africa, during one of his many adventures, von Rosen had collected many artefacts such as masks, skulls, and a magical drum said to have originated from a pygmy tribe in Central Africa. This drum, it was claimed, was used by the tribal shaman to contact the spirits of the tribe's forefathers. The artefacts, including the drum, were on display at von Rosen's castle, and one particular legend has it that the drum made horrible screaming sounds at night.

Another story involved the unusual rituals of the von Rosen family around a gigantic, thousand-year-old ash tree. This tree was so monumental in size that at the time it was measured it was declared the tallest tree in Northern Europe. Every new year von Rosen's family gathered around the tree where they drank mead from a medieval horn. They all pledged their vows for the coming year, and poured drops of mead on the roots of the tree, which they had named Yggdrasil. In northern myths and lore this is the name of the sacred ash tree, the world tree that carries the universe. At its roots, the Norns – the Norse equivalent of the Greek 'Fates' – weave the threads of the destinies of all people. Some say that because of these rituals, the tree on the von Rosen estate became magically linked to the vitality of the von Rosen family. The same night that Eric von Rosen became ill, lightning struck and split the tree in two, and when some time later Countess von Rosen passed away, a storm split the tree in halves again – or at least so the legends say. To this day von Rosen's ash tree still stands on the grounds of the eastern side of the castle.[5]

Count Eric von Rosen

Göring felt at home at Rockelstad Castle. After all, in his youth he had lived in a castle himself. Born on 12 January 1893 at the Marienbad sanatorium in Rosenheim, Bavaria, his father was Heinrich Ernst Göring, a former cavalry officer and first Governor-General of the German protectorate of South-West Africa (Namibia). His mother was Heinrich's second wife, Franziska Tiefenbrunn, a Bavarian peasant woman. At the time Hermann was born, his father was serving as consul-general in the land of voodoo: Haiti. His godfather was the wealthy physician and businessman Dr. Hermann Epenstein, a fierce Catholic Christian of Jewish descent. Although Göring sometimes claimed that his first name was in honour of Arminius, the legendary German chieftain who defeated the Roman legions at Teutoburg Forest, another version has it that he was named so in the memory of his godfather.

Epenstein supported the Göring family financially after Heinrich's death in 1913 and arranged for a small family home inside the old castle of Veldenstein near Nuremberg. It is rumored that Göring's mother became Epenstein's mistress for fifteen years, and that his younger brother Albert was the result of this illicit affair.

## The House of the Swastika

Rockelstadt Castle was a house of the swastika. It was here that Göring encountered this universal symbol for the first time, as he saw a number of swastikas adorning the iron grid on which blocks of wood were stapled in the huge hearth that dominated the hall of the castle.[6]

During his high-school years von Rosen had found swastikas on a Viking rune-stone on the Swedish island of Gotland. To the young Count who already possessed fierce nationalist tendencies, it was a Viking symbol. For his first expedition to South America in 1901 he had swastikas painted on his crates and luggage as he had chosen it to become his personal good luck sign. During a stay among the descendants of the Inca in Bolivia, he discovered their familiarity with and use of the swastika, and learned that the swastika was a universally known symbol. At his renovation of Rockelstad Castle in 1902 he used the swastika as decorative element. Green swastikas on a red background are found in the ceiling of the Great Hall, while for his hunting-lodge von Rosen commissioned architect Ivar Tengbom to design a set of furniture in the Old Nordic style, decorated with carved swastikas.[7]

The aeroplane that von Rosen had given to Finland in 1918 was also painted with swastikas on its wings before it was delivered. A large blue swastika on a white background subsequently became the emblem of the Finnish Air Force, and remained so until the end of World War II.

There has been some speculation that Göring was influenced by von Rosen's use of the swastika, and introduced the symbol to the Nazi movement in Munich, but this is not the case.[8] But on that night, something else of note did happen. While Hermann, Eric and his wife Mary sat in front of the fireplace engaged in conversation, a stately woman suddenly appeared and slowly descended the broad stairs to the hall. Tall and blonde, she embraced the Count and smiled at the pilot. To Göring, who was of the opinion that the most pure of all German blood was to be found in Sweden, she appeared as a Nordic-Germanic goddess. As he would later state, her blue eyes struck him like thunder.

Her name was Carin Fock, and she was there keeping her sister Mary, wife of Count Eric von Rosen, company. She was 32 years old, he was 27.[9] She was already married and had a son, but was estranged from her husband.

A passionate relation developed, and Carin soon divorced her husband and married Göring. She became the Nordic icon and cult figure of the bourgeoning Nazi party. Her nobility and his wartime achievements made them the perfect glamour couple to give the Nazi movement the much desired respectability and sophistication it desperately needed, far away from the beer-hall brawls and the thick necked, bare-fisted thugs of the early Nazi party.

Their marriage has been of great interest to those researching the possible influence of occult traditions on Nazism, as she introduced Göring to the mysterious Edelweiss Society that night, allegedly taking him on a tour of the family's private chapel devoted to the

Portrait of Carin Göring

society. Much has been written about the ominous influence of the Edelweiss Society on the birth of Nazism, with some accounts even going so far as to describe certain rituals that seem to be pure invention rather than historical truth.[10] As with much of the literature on Nazism and the occult, many of these 'histories' are highly inaccurate.

## The Mystic Sisterhood

A strain of exalted Christian mysticism, seership, mediumistic abilities and a penchant for the esoteric ran deep in the female side of the Fock family. Von Rosen's wife Mary von Rosen, elder sister of Carin Göring, was one of the founders of the Societas Sanctae Birgittae, a Lutheran High Church society in the Church of Sweden. She was the first Mother Superior from 1920 to 1964, three years before her death.[11]

Societas Sanctæ Birgittæ was founded in 1920 as a response to the decline of the Church of Sweden, involving amongst others a more ceremonial celebration of the Mass. Its founding was initiated by archbishop Nathan Söderblom, answering the need for a religious society for both men and women. Söderblom had introduced members of the Brotherhood of St Sigfrid to Count and Countess Eric and Mary von Rosen, who were passionate in their adherence to St Birgitta of Sweden. This 14th century saint and mystic is best known for writing books about her mystical visions of Jesus and Mary, and letters to many Church and political leaders. She is also one of the six patron saints of Europe. In 1909 Mary had erected a private chapel dedicated to her in one room in Rockelstad Castle. It was finished in 1917. The friezes of the tower room were painted with the nine revelations of St. Birgitta by Oscar Brandtberg, headmaster of the Royal Academy of Art, and a good friend of the von Rosens.

While one author identifies this as an Edelweiss chapel,[12] this was actually not so. There is ultimately some confusion as to which chapel exactly Göring was shown by Carin – elsewhere we read that Carin "showed him the tiny chapel of the family's private Edelweiss Order nestling behind the castle".[13] This was a chapel erected as a surprise by the daughters for their mother, and was situated in a former stable in the courtyard.

One can see though how this highly charged atmosphere of deeply felt Christianity created room for the type of mystical experience the Fock sisters underwent. Carin was said to have had, since early childhood, an acute sense of premonition. She was also deeply mystical. According to her sister, and earliest biographer, Fanny Gräfin von Wilamowitz-Moellendorff, writing in 1933...

> Carin lived all her life in two worlds... She was familiar with the world of heaven since early childhood. She had the gift of inner vision, she saw and heard much that others could not experience.

Inside the Edelweiss chapel

This gift she had in common with her mother. The bond was not only earthly, but also heavenly in nature. It often looked to me as if her guardian angel had laid a golden staff in her hands like a ray of sunlight, that connected the child's soul with heaven.

In her childhood she also 'felt' the emotional states of complete strangers, and knew beforehand when "someone was thinking or planning something bad".[14] A less hagiographic estimate of Carin's character has it that she had a liking for 'romantic-religious thought' which she had inherited from her mother: "The women in the Fock family were all domineering and eccentric. They were romantic… and like their mother they avoided banal reality."[15]

## The Edelweiss Gesellschaft

Fanny Gräfin von Wilamowitz-Moellendorff, Carin's sister, observed in her biography that there was "something in the Fock family about which not much was spoken to the outer world, that had for the inner life and for the home a profound meaning notwithstanding. That was, to be short and like the daughters used to say: 'mama and her Edelweiss chapel'."

> Some years before her death, the grandmother, Mrs. Beamish, had founded a small society that she had named after the mountain flower Edelweiss. Its members could belong to any faith, yet they had to oblige themselves to commit to charity in an absolutely selfless way. Seeing need meant to dissolve need. Being a visionary of the most rare kind, she believed in the prolongation of the divine revelations in the life of a single individual and in the lives of entire nations. To maintain this connection of the human soul with the eternal homeland and to possibly strengthen and renew it, was to her her holy duty. The members of the Edelweiss society had

to adhere to purity, truth and love, the source of strength being prayer and the absolute trust in god...

In order to come to terms with oneself and to create spiritual power and in order to keep alive the connection to the above, it is necessary to enter the silence. Mrs. Beamish knew from experience... how difficult it is to conquer this silence. In those days the churches in Sweden were closed during the weekdays... [and] to be left undisturbed in one's own home is rarely possible. Therefore she created a small chapel for the members of her society... a sanctuary for many a soulful and spiritually ambitious person. Now and then music was performed...many people got a better inner view of their character, their difficulties and possibilities in life. Many especially gifted persons became illuminated, became clairvoyant... From within advice would be given, intuitively one could sense the ways of divine providence, and through that serve lighter and better.[16]

In truth, the Edelweiss Society was founded in the 19th century by Huldine Beamish with the erection of a small chapel in a house in Stockholm. She also penned poetry under the pen-name 'Edelweiss'[17] and wrote a book on spiritism that saw an English translation.[18] As such her interests were typical of any intelligent woman of her day. The 19th century was the era of spiritual enlightenment, and some of the most influential esoteric and mystical movements – of which a number still exist today – were founded then. The role of women especially increased, as they struggled for emancipation – one has but to think of Anna Kingsford's descriptions of her hostile reception at the University of Paris when she went studying there. In the esoteric movements women found at least a measure of equality. Moreover, Stockholm had also seen the visionary revelations of Emanuel Swedenborg a century earlier.

The membership role of the early Edelweiss Society is impressive. Swedish artist Hilma af Klint briefly became a member. As a child she had shown a gift for mediumship and had experienced visions of the future, so she had come into contact with spiritualist circles in Stockholm at an early age. She also took part in organized spiritualist séances between 1879 – 1882. Her bequest includes a notebook, which shows that she was in contact with the Edelweiss Society. She joined in 1896, but left shortly afterwards, possibly because she found herself confronted by women as strong-willed and domineering as herself.[19] Another member was 19th century court photographer Bertha Valerius. In 1856 she began to work on a drawing entitled 'The Prince of Peace'. Untrained in art, she worked on it till 1896 when she completed it. The original drawing is said to have once hung in the Edelweiss chapel in Stockholm.[20] However, in the photo of the Edelweiss chapel in Carin Göring's biography, the drawing is absent. Obviously the Edelweiss Society was not at all that what certain writers on the theme of Nazism and occultism want it to be.

## Göring and Edelweiss: The Myth

It is clear that in Fanny's biography – which was published with the blessing of those in power in the Third Reich – the Edelweiss Society was hijacked for propaganda purposes. For instance one passage clarifies that…

> Those who have often seen Hermann Göring in civilian clothes, will have noticed, that he carries an Edelweiss flower on his hat. This flower has also become the flower of the Führer. The flower may serve as a remembrance to his beloved mountains, to that profound loneliness in the upper atmosphere above all pettiness and evanescence. The higher the wanderer ascends, the more rare flowers become. There above one has the view of the distance, the silence, the white mountains, heaven and the glitter of the sun. A

small white flower may give one luck for a long time. Proudly she wears her white crown at the edge of the abyss. She could cost him his life, but once he has conquered her, she appears to him more valuable than laurels or gold. Is it not a rare divine providence that that especially this flower, the Edelweiss, since early childhood on has been familiar and sacred to Carin?[21]

This may sound terribly important, and Carin Göring's biographer obviously had this objective in mind. However, the Edelweiss flower as a symbol for various nationalistic, political and social tendencies and movements stretches far beyond any connection between the Edelweiss Society and the Nazi movement, and this is well documented.[22] There even was for instance in the Third Reich a youth movement which fiercely opposed the Nazi regime, which called itself 'Edelweiss Piraten'.

Also, with the advent of Nazism in Germany and Göring's entanglement with it, a schism occurred between Mary von Rosen and Carin Göring In surviving letters from the 1920s, Carin writes how she met with Hitler and Mussolini and thought Hitler "the more genuine, especially a genius, full of truth, love and ardent faith". And elsewhere she writes to her mother with a revolutionary zeal, "Just know that Hitler thing is good." And with it came a nasty streak of anti-Semitism. She writes for instance about a Jewish doctor whom she had consulted: "he is so small and horrible to look at, but very good and I feel so grateful to him."[23] So much for her empathy, so passionately described by her biographer sister.

Mary von Rosen on the other hand, to whom the same tendencies of empathy and a strong sensibility are ascribed, thought and felt very differently. When she met the Führer, she got a spontaneous feeling of discomfort. Interviewed on this subject in the mid 1960s she explained how during her encounters with Hitler she saw him as "increasingly sinister", while her final meeting with him was a "psychological horror experience" for her.[24]

Carin Fock's divorce from her first husband in order to marry Göring had also met with disapproval from her family. Her letters were seldom answered, and as a consequence she felt dejected and isolated from her parents and grandmother.

Carin had heart problems, and at 42 years of age she was admitted to a sanatorium. In one of her last letters, she wrote how Jews were not allowed in the sanatorium. "[I]t is so nice and peaceful in this Jew-filled country", she wrote. The following year, in 1931, Carin Göring died of a blood clot.[25]

While Carin was a strong and active medium in the Edelweiss Society, she never was the leader. After Huldine Beamish died, leadership was transferred through the family line to Elsa Fock, and when she died a short time later, to Mary von Rosen. The simple truth is that Hermann Göring only encountered the Edelweiss Society indirectly and for the briefest of times; and his often quoted letter[26] to Huldine Beamish, where he describes the "wonderful short hour that he had in the chapel", really does not amount to as much as some would like to believe. The more prosaic view of Göring's letter would be that it simply shows a man in love, wanting to make a good impression on the mother of the object of his desire.

## Von Rosen's Sub Rosa

There is a curious postscript to the strange legends surrounding Eric von Rosen and his wife, as he in turn also had a remarkable person as grandmother.

This leads us to the other subject that has been associated with the 'secret history' of the Third Reich: its assumed search for alternative energy sources, free energy, and antigravity. Just as the 19th century saw a revival of the occult, new advances in science also saw an upsurge in unusual and avant-garde ideas and concepts in regards to a means of creating energy. It was the era of Nikola Tesla and his contemporary

John Worrell Keely. The secret history of the Third Reich is wrought with strange synchronicities and coincidences. Hermann Göring would become the head of the Luftwaffe, Nazi Germany's air force, and it was whispered that the Third Reich designed and built various disc-shaped aeroforms propelled by exotic technologies. On the other hand, John Keely had been experimenting with antigravity half a century before the advent of Nazi Germany.

In 1898, in Philadelphia, Keely passed away. Infamous even at the time for his supposed harnessing of "etheric" or "vibratory sympathy" forces, Keely's work was backed by a remarkable woman who would become his most staunch and loyal ally. She wrote many pamphlets and one book about Keely, and supported his research financially for more than fifteen years. Mrs. Bloomfield-Moore (maiden name Clara Sophia Jessup) was an extraordinary and highly intelligent woman with a deep interest in avant-garde science and the occult. She corresponded with many scientists in all parts of the world, including Tesla (whom she met at least once), Charles Howard Hinton (who had authored a number of books on the fourth dimension), and Hiram Maxim, early aviation pioneer and inventor of the Maxim gun. Her social circle included some of the most famous, wealthy and influential persons of her day, such as her acquaintance John Jacob Astor, who once was courted by Tesla to fund his research. She also developed a "long and intimate" relationship with Helena Blavatsky, the founder of Theosophy. Blavatsky published excerpts of her writings on Keely in her book *The Secret Doctrine*.

Bloomfield-Moore died only a few months after Keely; her literary executor, science writer Henry Dam, wrote of their close relationship:

> I knew that when Mr. Keely died she would not live long. Her whole life was centered in his work to the exclusion of all other interests and hopes. She had the most profound faith that neither Mr. Keely or herself could die until the invention had succeeded.

After receiving the cabled announcement of Keely's death she began to sink rapidly. Her ailment seemed more mental than physical.

Having been presented to the court of Queen Victoria, both her daughters married nobility. One daughter married the Swedish Baron Carl von Bildt. Her other daughter, Ella, married Count Carl von Rosen. A son resulting from this marriage was Count Eric von Rosen.

However, she was not a Theosophist, at least according to Count Eric von Rosen:

> No. She was interested in the study of Theosophy as a broad-minded woman. She was interested speculatively, but did not believe in it.

More than half a century after Keely's death his still-living nephew was located and interviewed. The old man recalled how Mrs. Bloomfield-Moore sent "many of Keely's secrets" to Count Eric von Rosen. He apparently sent this material to Stockholm in 1912, and nothing more was heard of these 'secrets'. Perhaps these consisted of the materials, mainly photographs of various engine-like devices with the handwriting of Mrs. Bloomfield-Moore on several of them, that were published in 1972 in Sweden.[27]

Years later I found an intriguing claim pertaining to certain experiments conducted in the Third Reich. Briefly, the context of these experiments was the search for alternative means of creating fuel for the German war machine, as Germany had no reserves of oil. But it did have large quantities of coal. It used a process called the Fischer-Tropsche method to create oil from gas. But there is a hint that there was another process in existence with which Nazi Germany allegedly was able to refine oil into various usable components using certain sound waves. Or so it was claimed by prisoner-of-war Josef Ernst to his English captors. The document in question, the British Intelligence Objectives Sub-Committee report number 142, reads in part:

Ernst claimed to have invented a process for the separation of petrol from oil by the use of vibrations of audible frequency. This method was developed from the Kelly process in use in the U.S.A. The crude oil is passed through glass tubes suspended above a plate of 'pertinax', which is caused to vibrate at frequencies on the Pythagoras tone-scale. The frequency is altered according to the product required… This process was operated at the wells near Hamburg owned by the S.S. and many tons of petrol were produced. These factories were probably destroyed, but the apparatus is possibly in the south of Germany.[28]

It is clear from the description of the method that by 'Kelly', free-energy researcher researcher John Worrell Keely and his 'sympathetic vibration' is meant – the man whose chief financial backer was the grandmother of Count Eric von Rosen.

**Theo Paijmans** has authored two books, a history of the UFO phenomenon published in 1996, and *Free Energy Pioneer: John Worrell Keely*. Published in 1998 it has been reprinted and saw a translated version published in Japan in 2000. His articles and papers have appeared in various publications including *All Hallows, Strange Attractor, The Anomalist, Gazette Fortéenne, The Centre for Fortean Zoology Yearbook 2009* and *Fortean Times*, where he is a regular columnist. His papers on the History of Spring-heeled Jack in America and Spring-heeled Jack in New Zealand were published in an academic collection under the editorship of Mike Dash. Theo was invited to speak and participate in the panel discussion at the 2008 Fortean Times Unconvention, and has recently appeared as expert in a Discovery Channel documentary on the Vril Society (*Dark Fellowships: The Vril Society*), the subject of his book slated to appear at a later date.

# The Starry Wisdom

## A Perichoresical Perambulation Through the Works of Kenneth Grant

by *Paolo Sammut*

Kenneth Grant (1924-2011) was one of the most noted magicians of the 20th century. Well known as Aleister Crowley's final student in the mid-1940s, he went on to develop his own interpretation of Thelema and take the Great Work through Yuggothian gateways and out towards wholly new starry dimensions. However despite his massive opus, he frequently received criticism and has (I feel unfairly) gained a reputation for being incomprehensible or worse. This misunderstanding has blighted perception of his writings and perhaps contributed to it having a slower uptake than it deserves, as a highly insightful body of work which forms a complex and interwoven commentary upon so many esoteric subjects.

By the end of his long writing career, Kenneth Grant had written an entire shelf of books, most notably the *Typhonian Trilogies*, which built upon the occult background radiation left behind by groups such as the Hermetic Order of the Golden Dawn and luminaries including Aleister Crowley, Jack Parsons and Dion Fortune. Extending his Typhonian Gnosis, he allowed concepts such as trafficking with entities, sexual gnosis and an entire nightside[1] tradition to seep into his novels which were often shorter works featuring a sidereal[2] connection to his own person, thus creating a strange symmetry where Kenneth Grant himself walked within his own fiction, and the beings and energies – and indeed the sense of *other* which he evoked – bled back from his prose into our reality. As many of his readers will note, there is a dreamlike, unnerving quality to Grantian fiction where the borderland of fact and fantasy dissolve into a compelling narrative where one is caught within the bindings and the firmament of the story.

This is all a part of his magic, and one of the reasons why his books are often described not so much as being about magic, but as being magical objects in their own right. This is their real value, as Grant enfolded magic into the very linguistic structure of his text, making it a jumping off point to other realities. I have certainly found this for myself, and reading his work late at night I am often lead into to a sense of reverie which mutates very easily into deeper states of meditative consciousness. Indeed, often the *Typhonian Trilogies* seem to transmute and reflect to the reader exactly what they *need* to read at that particular time to further their magical development.

Kenneth Grant did not write for beginners, and one will not find set rituals such as the *Lesser Banishing Ritual of the Pentagram* or the *Middle Pillar* within his books; rather one is expected to ponder over the information and accounts given and design one's own path through the mysteries which he so tantalizingly unveils. His writing style is unique, and very different from the formulaic precision we find with Aleister Crowley. Grant polarised Thelemites in that many people feel that has detracted from the spirit of what Crowley was trying to achieve. However in contrast to this, many people feel that Kenneth Grant, in following his own stars (not those of Aleister Crowley) opened new doors to insight, exploration and mystery. Furthermore, some of Grant's work is remarkably prescient regarding the effects on human consciousness from the universe at large. For example his commentary on UFOs in *Outer Gateways*[3] references and builds upon ideas suggested by Arthur Machen in *The Great God Pan*[4] and John Keel in books such as *The Mothman Prophecies*,[5] and describes a non-nuts-and-bolts model of UFOs from the esoteric perspective, a view which is really only recently becoming more prominent.

### Telepathic Transmissions from Yuggoth

One of the more problematic areas within Grant's corpus of writing is that which connects to HP Lovecraft's Cthulhu mythos. We know as a fact that HP Lovecraft made up this mythos, seeding it both with entities found in mythology (such as Dagon) and those that he invented (such as Yog-Sothoth or Hastur the Unspeakable). Furthermore Lovecraft was an ardent materialist, who in his letters frequently commented that it was all invented, using names such as the *Necronomicon* or *Abdul Alhazred* simply because he just liked the sound to that word. Finally, a scan of the literature shows that there are no reliable references to the *Necronomicon* or the made up entities prior to Lovecraft's stories being published.

In order to add authenticity to his stories Lovecraft created a fictional history of the *Necronomicon* which referenced real historical persons such as John Dee and Olaus Wormius, a scheme that 'went viral' as other authors continued adding to the mythos in subsequent years. It is remarkable that even recently, after the subject has been debunked to death and excellent books upon the subject such as

*The Necronomicon Files*[6] have appeared – which clearly present in a well referenced manner the facts of the case – there are still people accepting the literal truth of HP Lovecraft's blasphemous confection.

How then are we to unify these facts with the knowledge that Kenneth Grant referenced the *Necronomicon* throughout his work from the beginning? Grant was a true scholar and very well read, as the list of references in the back of his books testify, so we can be certain that he was aware of the mundane non-history of the *Necronomicon* and that – on our level at least – it is all fiction. In fact he acknowledges that Lovecraft invented the *Necronomicon* in the beginning chapter of *Outer Gateways*. In Grant's words:

> A number of arcane texts claiming non-terrestrial provenance are of supreme significance in the sphere of creative occultism. Perhaps the most mysterious and certainly the most sinister is the Necronomicon, the first mention of which appears in the fiction of the New England writer H. P. Lovecraft. Said to have been written by a mad Arab named Al Hazred, the Necronomicon actually exists on a plane accessible to those who, either consciously like Crowley, or unconsciously like Lovecraft, have succeeded in penetrating it.[7]

This paragraph succinctly sums up everything that Kenneth Grant has to say on the *Necronomicon*. He is clear that H.P. Lovecraft made it up, and equally clear that he believes that Lovecraft's work was being enthused from a deeper level of reality. Indeed, the Necronomicon; as a primal grimoire; is a source of inspiration throughout all of Grant's primary work, beginning with *The Magical Revival*[8] where Grant lists a number of correspondences between Lovecraftian Mythos Lore and Thelema.

Since then Grant has added to the number of connections using gematria[9] with names and words found in other traditions, not least Aleister Crowley's *Book of the Law*. This has included connecting words which have a linguistic or gematrical similarity to terminology

Cover for Grant's *The Magical Revival*

found in the Mythos, such as "Set-Hulu" or "Tutulu" - a word heard by Crowley whilst scrying the Enochian Aethyrs in the Sahara desert in 1909 with the poet Victor Neuberg[10] – which Grant relates to *Cthulhu*. Throughout the later volumes, Grant references the Necronomicon in the same manner that he references other traditional sources such as Gnostic, Hebrew and Sanskrit. This theme continues throughout the Trilogies, however I feel that it reaches its climax in the erudite *Hecate's Fountain* where Grant speaks of rituals to summon Cthulhu – and it is here that we find the mentioned comparison between the *Book of the Law* and the *Necronomicon*.

But returning to the question as to whether the mythos is literally real, we might best answer it by comparing it to humanities other 'accepted' ancient traditions. All myths, religions and spiritual practices start with a mystic contacting the ineffable and building a link. So maybe we need to look at HP Lovecraft himself. Although a materialist and sceptic on the outside, Grant suggests that Lovecraft may have been an unconscious seer who could perceive deeper patterns of reality, although being uninitiated to their true nature, he would then shy away with fear. Certainly a lot of Lovecraft's tales originated in dreaming, and some tales were almost exact recounts of his dreams, illustrating that their origin was not from his regular dayside consciousness, but at the very least an unconscious source separate from his wakeful materialism. However, even if Lovecraft consciously made up the mythos, this does not break the validity of Kenneth Grant's connection to it. Grant would recognise the familiar mystical patterns that Cthulhu and the Great Old Ones fall into and weave his practice around this. All myths and religions started in a similar way, and in this sense the mythos is as real and valid as any other mythology and religion, albeit one from our repressed collective unconsciousness.

Perhaps we could understand this idea more if we consider a fictional storyteller who is creating a new serial killer character for a novel. They would use certain patterns and archetypes in their creation of the character with their origin in the behaviour of real serial killers. As such our virtual serial killer is a symbol for the spirit of serial killings which underlies the madness in all the ones we encounter (or hopefully not) in our world. So in a sense a fictional Hannibal Lector, properly realised, is as real as Jack the Ripper and Ted Bundy.

## Taking a Walk on the Night Side

From here perhaps we could ask why one would *want* to encounter night-side entities such as Cthulhu. I believe that Grant's work has an unfairly gained reputation for being overly dark, and that perhaps this reputation is due to 'fluffy-bunny' occultists not really understanding that the Universe (and by extension ourselves) is composed of both light and darkness. It is vital to carefully (and safely) explore these energies, since on one level they are out there and nasty, but they are also within us and potential. Remember Freud's ideas of the need to express, then assimilate repressions; in a magical sense this is why one faces the darkness, to bring it into the light rebirthed as a wholesome energy rather than left as a repressed dark time bomb ready to explode. A lot of Grant's work here is really an insightful glimpse into the Theosophic concept of the Dweller on the Threshold – and serious occultists do not work with the dark-side to harm, but rather to regenerate their own darker repressions into the light of a loving self.

The highest grade of occultism according to the Hermetic Order of the Golden Dawn is "Ipsissimis" which means "one's self complete": one has healed and assimilated all one's fractures, all one's broken parts, all one's personal demons into a perfect being in knowledge of their true (unified) will. This is more potent and far more healing than meditating upon dolphins and unicorns, and I feel that to misunderstand "dark" as being creepy and scary is to totally miss the ideas in Kenneth Grant's writing, which in actuality shows him to be one of the sanest occultists out there. In that respect, the mythos serves perfectly as a vehicle for these ideas.

## ALEISTER CROWLEY MEETS DRACULA AND THE MUMMY

Strange, eldritch fiction was very important to Kenneth Grant, and his use of the Lovecraftian mythos clearly shows that he saw it as a vessel capable of transmitting deep esoteric ideas. Many occultists testify that the occult novel often serves as a better conveyer of ideas than the occult textbook, and Grant himself embraced this concept. For example, Grants own novella *Gamaliel*[11] shows how clearly he understood the *occult* concept of vampirism, as opposed to the somewhat stereotypical Eastern European in a dinner jacket and Bela Lugosi smile. Grant (in *The Magical Revival*) traces vampirism back to ancient Egypt, referencing black magic practices designed to maintain the earth-bound part of the soul (the *ka*) to the service of a necromancer (utilising this bound *ka* as a familiar), although the original practice was to protect the tombs of the dead. This is a theme also explored by Dion Fortune in *The Demon Lover*,[12] however Fortune approaches it slightly differently given that her fictional "vampire" was not properly dead in the first place!

In the *Typhonian Trilogies* we see vampirism expounded as a transaction of energy with a deeper level which can lead to a depletion of vitality, of life and of being, with the host and the vampire both exchanging something – usually resulting in the persistence of the vampire and the diminution of the host.

Both Aleister Crowley and Austin Osman Spare dipped their toes into the subject of Vampirism in their writing; Grant however jumped right into the pool, clothes and all. Indeed, the subject is central to a theme found throughout Grant's work, the idea of 'stellar gnosis'. One of the historical threads which Grant explores is that of Queen SobekNoferu, who historically ruled Egypt for four years at the end of the 12th Dynasty, leading Egypt out of the Middle Kingdom period. We know very little about the historical SobekNoferu, however her name (which means "Beloved of Sobek") suggests a connection with the Egyptian crocodile god Sobek.

This connection forms part of the origin myth of the Typhonian tradition, which looks back into antiquity and early religious practices connecting humanity with our Goddesses. Dion Fortune in *Moon Magic*[13] alluded to a similar tradition, and the idea of civilisations predating Egypt in the Nile region is still something considered today via the controversial research by the likes of John Anthony West and Robert Schoch and their revised dating of the Great Sphinx. Grant saw SobekNoferu as a revivalist who brought through this tradition from deep antiquity into closer antiquity:

> The oracle is ThERA,[14] Queen of the Seven Stars who reigned in the Thirteenth Dynasty as Queen Sebek-nefer-Ra. She was it who brought over from an indefinitely ancient past, prior even to Egypt, the original Typhonian Gnosis.[15]

The Hammer House of Horror interpretation of Bram Stoker's *Jewel of the Seven Stars* (as *Blood from the Mummy's Tomb*) oozes pure 1950s elegance with the half-naked Valerie Leon as the (un)mummified and still vital and highly sexy corpse of Tera[16] surviving through the centuries to revive in modern times; a more modern and occult take on Bram Stokers tale, and once more true to the sidereal legacy of Grant and Austin Osman Spare and perhaps capturing some of the Nu-Isis ambience which Kenneth Grant was steeped in during the 1960s. In my view this is the most Typhonian film ever made; albeit slightly less accurate (on an archaeological level) than other films of the story,[17] but one can easily slip into a state watching the film where the learned Kenneth Grant steps out of the shadows to explain the narrative (in fact he practically does in the early volumes of his Trilogies).

I think that part of the importance to Kenneth Grant regarding Queen Sobek-Nefer-Ra is that she is female. Aleister Crowley whilst brilliant in his way; was an iconoclast who moved occultism forward in the difficult formative years of the twentieth century. However he was basically a Victorian gentleman with I feel some misogynistic tendencies which persisted into his teaching. It is clear from his writings that he saw his *scarlet women* as subservient to his work and that they all had roles within his path. In fact one of the reasons why I do not think that Aleister Crowley had much influence on Gerald Gardner during the formation of the Wicca movement is that Crowley certainly was not the sort to submit to a Priestess; all that is from Gardener.

Aleister Crowley

Kenneth Grant however is much more balanced in his writings, and avoids the pitfalls of both Crowley and Gardner in giving equal merit to both male and female mysteries in his work, recognising that both sexes add in their own way to initiation and the moving forward of the magical current. In Kenneth Grant's work we read about esotericism from both a male and a female perspective and important themes such as Kalas are introduced and developed.

## The Twilight between Fiction and Fact

Strange experiences move throughout Kenneth Grants work as part of a deeper weave with provides connections to these occurrences. These often begin as weird events which are described and then later developed in subsequent books often growing in a tangential fashion as Grant attaches these manifestations to different concepts.

Once such thread concerns the statue of Mephistopheles (affectionately nicknamed "Mephi" by Grant) which we first find mentioned in *Hecate's Fountain* as a statue which Kenneth bought from Busche's emporium on Chancery Lane, a premise which seems to have flourished before the Second World War. This statue seemed to have had a life of its own, apparently following Grant home rather than being purchased in the more traditional manner, with Grant finding a short while later, upon attempting to return the statue discovers that the emporium had closed.[18] A little later in *Hecate's Fountain*[19] we find that Mephi finds his way into a Nu-Isis rite of Oolak (one of the *Great Old Ones* of Grant's system) and serves to ground the powers raised in the rite. Mephi then pops up mysteriously in the novella *Against the Light* as an illustration on the cover, as well as being referenced in the book where Grant gives us a account of the purchase of the statue. All this may sounds rather strange and unlikely, however odd things do happen like this to occultists, and some objects enthused with presence do seem to often have a purpose of their own. I feel that the accounts of Mephi, in all Kenneth Grant's books, represent strange happenings which really occurred whilst he owned the statue.

My favourite novel by Kenneth Grant is *Against the Light*, which I feel is an absolute gem (it is worth noting that the 'Against' of the title means *next to*, as if with a lover, and certainly not *opposed to* or suggesting diabolical black magic). *Against the Light* is woven through with threads from Grant's own past; as noted he mentions the dealer in Charing Cross Road in London from where he obtained his statue of Mephistopheles; there are references to the (maybe fictional) *Grimoire Grantino*, fictional personages from various strange tales such as Helen Vaughan and a constant blurring of fiction and reality. This is all to the good since it leaves us all wondering what reality actually is. Perhaps the truth is that it is all fiction; all true. Perhaps our own lives are all fiction, all truth. The borderline haziness is where the magician, the artist and the poet all stand within their own cadences – and it is clear that Grant was all these, and perfectly comfortable in this twilight zone.

The noted writer and magician Alan Moore wrote a playful and erudite review[20] of this book which I understand Kenneth Grant liked very much. In his review Moore describes the value and power of Grant's novels as emerging from their unique place between fact and fiction. Here, framed in fiction, we see magic pour into our dimension infusing all it touches.

Grant is simultaneously extremely playful yet deadly serious. Oolak (mentioned above) is a form of Count Orlok from *Nosferatu*.[21] Again, like the Lovecraftian connection through which Grant explored vampirism in ritual these fictional nodes can serve as entrances for the energies which underlie their existence. Grant gives few hints in his work regarding exactly how he worked, and to understand more of this we need to read between the lines and engage in some speculation. We read some fantastic accounts in the books, such as the following from *Hecate's Fountain*, which gives the greatest number of accounts of the practices which the Nu-Isis lodge carried out. Most wonderfully we read on page 53 of the Skoob edition:

> The lodgeroom was prepared to exhibit the snowy vastness of that abominable plateau, situation in astral regions which coincide terrestrially with certain regions of Central Asia not precisely specified by Al Hazred. The walls and floor were white, and white were the seven coffins ranged upon trestles before a dazzlingly white altar where snowdrifts sparkled and traced upon the ice-smooth slopes of three pyramids…[22]

Clearly we need to read descriptions such as this with a careful eye and realise that Grant is not talking about some decoration in an upstairs spare bedroom! Whilst there may have been some physical decoration in their place of working (given the artistic talents of both

Kenneth and Steffi Grant), it is doubtful that a room for magical working would be so big. A further clue however is suggested from the following account:

> The lodgeroom was prepared for the performance of a type of lycanthropic and necromantic sorcery associated with two specific tunnels of Set. Imagine therefore, a miniature through more complex version of the Dashwood caves with – in lieu of the various grottoes provided for sensual dalliance – a serious of shell-shaped cells, like petrified vortices, designed with the sole purpose of attracting into their convolutions the occult energies of Yuggoth, and focusing them through the kalas of Nu Isis, represented by a gigantic vesica-shaped prism. The décor was weird in the extreme, the illuminations cunningly arranged to impart a sinister and shifting play of light and shade combined with audible images suggestive of rushing waters and whistling astral winds; an altogether eerie atmosphere created by a few deft touches of supreme artistry.[23]

Notice the use of words and phases such as *imagine* and *astral winds*. Such terminology is suggestive that these settings were imagined in the minds of the participants of the work. This is not as strange as one would expect since skills in visualisation are crucial to occult work, and it is within the minds-eye that phenomena is seen. We are all familiar with the idea of a memory palace, where a building is visually committed to memory as a collection of anchor points holding specific objects in their locus. Exactly the same thing is happening here and Grant, whilst writing in an evocative way, is I believe describing how the participants of Nu-Isis lodge would begin their work by creating an internal "vision space" as a mental location, ready to contact the entities which were the subject of the ritual in progress.

## On Stranger Tides

One of the most notable themes within Kenneth Grant's body of work is his recognition of the work of other occultists as they tap into the current of magical work which he describes. Most notable of these superstars was of course the occult artist Austin Osman Spare, who was a close friend of both Kenneth and Steffi Grant right up until his death in 1956. It is well worth obtaining a copy of *Zos Speaks*[24] by Grant, which details the communication between himself and Spare, as well as publishing Spare's grimoire *The Book of Zos vel Thanatos*. It has often been noted that without Kenneth Grant continually championing his work, there is a danger that Spare would have been forgotten by now. Certainly Spare, in being somewhat reclusive, had faded from the public limelight by the time he had met Kenneth Grant and his return to prominence only really began in 1975 when Grant's *Images and Oracles of Austin Osman Spare*[25] was published. We have come a long way from the monochromatic images found in this almost-40-year-old book, to the beautifully talismanic books that modern publishers such as Starfire and Fulgur produce today, in which we can see Austin Spare's glorious artwork lavishly reproduced in full high definition colour.

Another notable occultist brought to prominence by the work of Grant is Michael Bertiaux, whose work is recently undergoing a renaissance thanks to the reprint of his famously obscure and previously unobtainable *Voudon Gnostic Workbook*.[26] We also have Nema (mentioned in the Trilogies as Soror Andahadna), whose channelled piece *Liber Pennae Praenumbra* beautifully evokes the best of Thelema, speaking of a magical universe so much greater than us, full of mystery and wonder.

In Grant's later books we even see reference to the late Andrew D. Chumbley, whose reboot of traditional witchcraft in his *Azoëtia*[27] harks back to some of the themes developed by Austin Spare in "The Witches Sabbath". There are many other references to emerging occultists in Grant's work, and there can be little doubt his endorsement helped bring these writers to the attention of both occultists, and in some cases, the wider public.

Kenneth Grant's writings have been published since the 1960s, and until his recent passing, there has always been a new book to eagerly await. Alan Moore asks in his review of *Against the Light*,[28] "why do most occultists that I know, myself included, have more or less everything that Grant has ever published resting on our shelves?" Despite his passing, his influence continues to grow and we are already seeing work by writers enriched by the *Typhonian Trilogies* move into the day-side – for example, the English experimental group English Heretic produced an album called *Tales of the New Isis Lodge*[29] which playfully choreographs the accounts in *Hecate's Fountain* to music and the weird fiction found in literature and cinema such as the original *The Mummy*,[30] Lovecraft's *Fungi from Yuggoth*[31] and *Invasion of the Body Snatchers*[32] which inspired Grant.

Sadly the last title published was the recent *Grist to Whose Mill*,[33] which ironically was Kenneth Grant's first novel, written in the early 1950s, but which has only just now emerged from the publishing darkness into the light. It is sad that we shall see no more wonderful, magical books by Kenneth Grant, although his work shall live on and grow in our hearts, minds and souls.

**Paolo Sammut** is a U.K.-based researcher primarily interested in esoteric and paranormal subjects. His main areas of focus include Ceremonial Magic especially Enochiana and the Typhonian tradition, Spagyric Alchemy, Psychic Questing and Paranormal research. He lives in Somerset with a coterie of cats and his scarlet woman – herself a sorceress of no mean ability. Paolo sporadically maintains a blog on http://liminalwhispers.blogspot.co.uk/.

"Come Little Children" by Woraya Chotikul (cottonvalent.deviantart.com/). CCA3.0 Lice

# KILLING SLENDERMAN

### Editing a Modern Myth Before it Bites

by *Ian 'Cat' Vincent*

The Slenderman. A very modern monster. Born a mere three years ago in an internet Photoshop competition on the *Something Awful* website, this tall, suit clad, faceless entity rapidly spawned a dizzyingly complex mythology, growing from countless photo manipulations, acclaimed YouTube video series and blogs. Within weeks of his creation, terms like 'tulpa' were being used to describe him. Perhaps inevitably, his influence leaked from the fictions and Alternate Reality Games that were his home, into the fears and nightmares of many.

As Slenderman's fame spreads, it is perhaps time to consider – if this creature can manifest from the imaginal realms into our reality… can we fight it? If so – how?

## A Slender Thread

"Is this the real life? Is this just fantasy?"
– Freddie Mercury, *Bohemian Rhapsody*

"Magic is a disease of language."
– Aleister Crowley

On 6th November 2009, the paranormal-based radio talk show Coast To Coast AM received a series of phone calls from young people who were expressing concern about a creature that they had begun to fear. Several of the callers reported seeing (both in nightmares and reality) a tall, thin, faceless entity who utterly terrified them.

They were reporting sightings of Slenderman.

At this point (September 2012), the Slenderman phenomenon is just over three years old. In the year since I first wrote about him in *Darklore Volume 6*, his 'popularity' has only expanded. Aside from the countless blogs and vlogs (video blogs), two low-budget movies about him (*Hylo* and *Entity*) have been filmed. A book considering Slenderman's significance, by the Fortean writer Robin Snope (*The Paranormal Pastor*), has been published. A popular independent computer game, *Slender*, is entirely based on the player having to elude Slenderman in a dark forest…and, in keeping with the vast majority of the mythos, players have no way to fight him. All they can do is run.

In my previous piece on the subject, I ended with this question:

> On the internet, nobody knows if you're a dog. Or a tulpa. And if enough people describe something as a thought-form… could this collective imagining actually make that form manifest?

> And… if that form does manifest – this powerful, terrifying, unkillable thing called Slenderman – how can we fight it?

Considering the sheer ingenuity of the hundreds of writers and creators involved in the Slenderman project, it is no surprise that this question has already been considered in depth.

An important aspect to remember when looking into the Slenderman phenomenon is that it is, pretty much from the very start, a deeply metatextual thing. The vast majority of blogs refer to other blogs and stories within the corpus – treating them as possessing varying levels of veracity. For example: one of the earliest YouTube series, *EverymanHYBRID*, started as (supposedly) a series of amateur exercise/health videos, in which someone planted a Slenderman reference as a joke based on the earlier *Marble Hornets* series…which the *EH* characters originally considered to be fiction. This brought them to the attention of the 'real' Slenderman – with tragic results.

Though the high-profile YouTube series get a lot of the attention and are perhaps most responsible for the wider dissemination of the Slenderman mythos, it's the simple written blogs that tend to provide much of the underlying structure of the mythos. Here again, the other stories of the Slenderman may be taken as either fact or fiction – while (of course) maintaining the illusion that their own blog is a record of actual reality. And sometimes there are crossover events – tales which are told across a group of collaborating storytellers within the larger mythos.

In regards to trying to find ways to combat the threat of Slenderman within that shared universe, one influential series of blogs came to examine the possibility of fighting Slenderman on his own turf. Let us assume, they said, that Slenderman is a tulpa, a thought-form created out of fiction, manifesting in our reality. Could that actually be a weakness? Can that fact be used to fight, even destroy him?

The model of anti-Slenderman action which came out of those blogs is known as 'Core Theory'.

## Core Theory

One of the earliest influences on what eventually became Core Theory was a blog called *The Tutorial*. It's told from the perspective of a character known simply as 'M'. The first blog entry begins:

> This is is all because of fucking *Something Awful*.
> Fuck *Something Awful*.
>
> It all started out so fun. Let's make paranormal images, let's share them, try to find where I doctored this picture! Yay yay yay! Hide a ghost, find a ghost, watch other people find your ghost. Fun. A good way to kill 3 hours. It's weird to think it was only a year ago. Almost summer vacation. Everything was hot and sticky. People wanted to go to the mall, and I hated the mall so I stayed in and watched the nerdy horror thread and talked to other people who were doing the same. Fucking around the internet, looking for something to scare them. Then he posted it. The 1st pictures with it hidden away in forests and near kids and after fires. Can you find the Slenderman?
>
> Great stories were posted. People made awesome pictures. That forum was more popular then ever. I woke up, checked my emails, went on twitter, checked that thread, every morning like clockwork. Sometimes there would be new stuff and sometimes there wouldn't, but still it was great. People were being creative, people were making a new story, and, most importantly, people were scared.
>
> Then *Marble Hornets* came out. And the other blogs and videos, and everything started. So much stuff. So many people thinking about Slenderman. So many people fearing it. So many people writing about Slenderman.

Have you ever heard of The Philip Phenomenon? In the 70s a group of people in Canada literally thought a ghost into existence. It took months. They would sit around a table and think about Philip and make up stories about him and try to will him into existence. And then they did.

It became Him.
It was fun until it wasn't.
Until my brother died.

This isn't a blog about how weird stuff will start happening to me, then I get paranoid, then I start to hear about Slenderman from other people and don't believe you until it's too late and He's sitting right in front of me eating a cookie and I'm screwed. That already happened to me. And I survived. Because I was smart, I learned the rules, I kept moving. That's what this blog is, a way to teach people how to win against Him. Because I don't know how many of these Slenderman blogs are real or not (fun fact: you can tell a Slenderman blog/vlog isn't real if it completely copies *Marble Hornets*, which is most of them), but I'm tired of seeing all these people make the same mistakes over and over.

The same mistakes I made.
The same mistakes that got my brother killed.

M goes on to establish the rules by which he has managed to survive and elude Slenderman thus far. They are:

1. *Get up high.* (M has noted that Slenderman appears not to be able to see him when he's above ground level. Even a few yards up a tree or on a roof is enough.)
2. *Keep moving.*
3. *Keep your eyes open.*

As the blog progresses, it becomes clear that others, writing in the comments section, are trying to apply M's rules to their own situation. Then, other commenters start to talk about trying to find ways to actually fight, rather than flee, Slenderman.

The first blog to gain popularity with a tale about actually opposing Slenderman was *Seeking Truth*. The narrator, 'Zeke Strahn', is, as they say on *The Wire*, Natural Police – a detective investigating a series of child disappearances, who is dragged into the understanding that the abductions are not simply caused by a human assailant. After enduring terrible losses (a child in his care, and his partner and occasional lover Lizzie) and a direct encounter with Slenderman, Zeke gets his rage on...

> Little Miss Lizzie
> was having a tizzy
> while eating her curds and whey.
> A long Slender spider
> tried to sat down beside her
> but then I came and blew the fucker away
>
> ...That's the story I'm working on right now.
>
> It's still a rough draft, but...I don't know, I think it has a nice ring to it, don't you?

Before going to face what may be his final confrontation with Slenderman, Zeke leaves the following post (23 July 2010):

> And here is my message to the people out there, reading this, fighting him:
>
> I know at the end of the blogs, they tell you that when the time comes that he comes after you, that you should end it yourself.

Take your own life so that he doesn't take it. Well today, I tell you the opposite.

Don't quit.
Don't give up.
Fight.
Fight him as long and as hard as you can.
He may win in the end.
But don't give him the satisfaction of an easy kill.
Let the fucker work for his food.

You can't keep letting him think that just because he holds the royal flush that it means you have to just fold. If enough people fight, if enough people give him a good run around…it may be enough to finish him.

So please.
Don't give up.
Give it everything you've got.

"Slenderman" by 'Kaptyn-Querq' (kaptyn-querq.deviantart.com/)
CCA3.0 Non-Derivative Licence

If you have to end it before he gets you, then do it.
But give it your all before you do.

Give him one hell of a show before you do.

Many commenters on both *The Tutorial* and *Seeking Truth* warmed to the idea that Slenderman can actually be fought – suggestions on how to do so range from such classic anti-supernatural tools as salt and cold iron, to more straightforward weapons (swords, guns, baseball bats, even fire extinguishers) or powers (water, fire, electricity).

Some, however, rather than trying to find ways to strike at any particular manifestation or (to use a computing term) instance of Slenderman, consider the possibility of striking decisively at the heart of the Slenderman phenomenon instead. Using the Tulpa Effect itself as a weapon.

Key among these is a man called Robert Sagel (the creation of writer Grady J. Gratt). Sagel thinks the fictional origin of Slenderman can be used, aikido-like, against him. And in his own blog, *White Elephants* (begun in September of 2010), he starts to explain how.

Sagel's plan is create an opposing force to Slenderman, derived from (a rather mangled version of) C.G. Jung's archetype theory. He designates himself and other bloggers certain key roles, bestowing upon them titles which reflect their actions and define which archetype they are to represent. Then, once the group is working together, he hopes they can literally rewrite the story of Slenderman – to turn it into a tale in which Slenderman can now be defeated.

The names and definitions of these archetypal figures are summed up by the *Slenderbloggins* OOG blog (Out-Of-Game – i.e. looking at the Slenderblogs as fictions rather than playing along) as follows:

> **Sage**: There's a dark jungle next to the village. People who go into it never return. The villagers fear the jungle. Then one day a man with a torch goes in, the villagers scream at him to not, but he does anyway.

He returns the next night, crawling back, bleeding to death, claw marks on his back. With his last breath he says 'Within the Jungle lives a Tiger, who is twelve feet long, obsidian claws, and has fire in its eyes...but it is just a Tiger and it bleeds.' After that he dies. The villagers no longer fear the jungle after that day. Oh, it's still scary and they take precautions from the huge Tiger...but it's just a Tiger. No longer is it Unknown or Shadows, perhaps one day someone will go and kill the Tiger...but there is no need for pointless fear.

**Mystic:** The Mystic can equal to -Veteran.- Mystic has fought, stores the knowledge of the past, and continues to give support when possible.

**Hermit:** The Hermit lives by himself, has developed methods to survive, and is willing to pass on instructions, but has his own priorities, and odds are will not fight as opposed to run.

**Warrior:** Brave, Bold, Stupid in that headstrong way, Fights for the sake of the fight, Fights without fear, Only fights on This Side, Can push /Construct/ back to Other Side for a while, cannot beat it. A stop gap, and if they become an /Agent/ then there's going to be a lot of trouble. [*Note: /Construct/ means Slenderman itself. /Agent/ means someone possessed or controlled by Slenderman – sometimes also known as a Proxy. This Side and the Other Side refer to our world and the Slender Man's world, respectively.*]

**Guardian:** Calm, controlled with knowledge, Fights for others BUT will have nothing left on This Side, Fights on Other Side, Stays on Other Side and keep Him there for a much longer time, will return when the Vigil is over, or if a Hero emerges.

**Hero:** Afraid but pushes on, Foolish but gains wisdom from Sages and Mystics, Fights for those who are important to him, Fights on both This Side and Other Side Only a Hero can kill a monster... but the Hero always dies at the end of the story.

As the *Slenderbloggins* piece also notes:

> There were a total of six Sages: Robert (*White Elephants*), Jay (*Anomalous Data*), and Shaun (*Testing, 1 2 3*) made up the first generation, while Zero (*A Hint of Serendipity*), Maduin (*A Really Bad Joke*), and Amelia (*Road to the Heavens*) made up the second generation.
>
> The title of Mystic was given to Zeke Strahm. This is where the title of his second blog comes from.
>
> The title of Hermit went to M.
>
> The title of Warrior was never given, but Robert implied that it belonged to Zeke before he became the Mystic.
>
> The title of Guardian was taken by Robert after he passed on the title of Sage.
>
> The title of Hero was never filled.

*White Elephants*, and the group of blogs that Sagel referenced, are notable for the considerable back-and-forth (in character, and within each respective version of the mythos) in their comments sections. Nominees for archetypal figures discuss their plans, while proxies and other servants of Slenderman try to dissuade and attack them. Some of the bloggers note that being associated with an archetype-name seems to assist their own efforts – in some cases, possibly providing actual defences or even special abilities related to them.

One of these commenters – the character 'Zero' of the blog *A Hint of Serendipity* (one of my personal favourites in the corpus) – proposes a specific plan to the other nominated bloggers: that they co-ordinate their efforts against Slenderman into a single push, focussed on one event on a specific date – the Winter Solstice of 2010.

Zero had an advantage over many of the other victims of Slenderman in that he was already an experienced role-play gamer – this gave him the option of modelling his experiences, and those of other victims, from the perspective of gaming. (The metatexturality of doing this within an Alternate Reality Game is notable.) His insights were valuable, especially to the growing Core Theory named participants.

An early example:

> /Construct/ was created by a gap in social conscience, I think. We've heard people blame [*Something Awful*] for its existence, which can sound laughable, but perhaps is more true than we thought. *Something Awful*, while I do not visit it, is well known as being a very culture-centric site. As I understand it, a great deal of memes are created there, that spread out into the internet culture.
>
> When the communication explosion occurred, back when texting and facebook started, we stumbled across something magical, the ability for instant communication gratification. Stimulus/Response from practically anywhere in the world, at your fingertips. Added with the mobility of cell phones, this staggered us as a culture. People were killed responding to texts while driving, lives crumbled, and school rooms were simple texting grounds. These things still happen, but now we're starting to step up against it. Communication evolved farther than our ability to understand it, we needed to grow socially, as the whole world, to understand what we had done.

One of the games I've played has a concept of magic that in essence says, 'the more you're taught something, the more you're defined as to what your world is, the less potential you have, because you've chosen to rigorously define what is and is not real.' I've seen this as a sound theory, and while I am naturally skeptical of things, I believe that this could in fact be the case. What was it Sherlock Holmes said? "If you take away the impossible, whatever remains, however improbable, must be the truth."

This malaise, this cultural reawakening we discovered, threw back the curtains, and revealed to us another truth, and for a few years, we were children, open to the fantastic yet again. This is how we got here.

So here's my proposal. We need to kill him, here on-line together. We all need to write a story, a paragraph at least, of how the /constructs/ die, and leave us rid of them forever. We need to tap into that morass, and spread the word, get it on *Something Awful*, maybe make it a contest or something, where everyone submits a story, and kill this asshole in our minds and spirits. Do it, Kill the Slender Man!

As more and more of the Core Theory group were targeted by Slenderman's Agents in-game, pressure grew to find a specific plan of attack. Suggestions from *The Tutorial* and other blogs implied that Slenderman was perhaps slightly weaker at the Solstices. With the Winter Solstice fast approaching, Zero proposed to the Core Theory group the following plan:

On the 21st of December 2010, Zero and several other bloggers would lead a direct physical attack against Slenderman, after luring him to a specific location. The intent would not be to actually kill Slenderman – instead, they simply intended to wound him, *to show others that it was possible to do so*. The secondary aspect of the attack would be to encourage other bloggers to write stories of this attack from their own perspective – whether they were present within the battlespace or not. It would be these stories – all conforming to the broad description of the event as told later by the participants, but each with their own *Rashamon*-like variations, which would install an ongoing weakness into the Slenderman mythos as a whole... leading to the rise of a later Hero-archetype, who would thus have a much better chance of fully defeating Slenderman. As Zero wrote in his final post before the Solstice Event:

> I've said before, that you are the key to victory. You always have been. What I need you all to do is simply write a story about what happens. It's that simple. I've given instructions to the people who are attending the Event to elaborate and romanticize the entire deal, to let fantasy add its mark to the fight. All of you readers who are not attending, I will ask you, as well, to write a story. Tell in your own words what you think happens.
>
> So now that I've intentionally shed confusion on most observers, everyone has a more equal amount of credibility for writing. As I said, some of you said you're coming, but do not have the address I am at. Some of you, I spoke to but have not alluded to showing. Others are just reading this now, and have never left their homes. It's because of this unreliable narrator quality, we can discuss on equal terms what happens.
>
> Why should you do this for me? Because this is how we kill the monster. We, as a blogosphere, discuss, critique, and solidify a story of this Event, enough that we can agree and deem it canon. It doesn't matter what is true within it or not. The point is that we progress further into the chain of events, advancing another rung closer to killing the Slender Man. In a literal sense, I am putting my life on the line, that you readers and bloggers can come together to give a cohesive answer as to the happenings today.

The Solstice Event went more-or-less as planned. Participants from many blogs, from the Core Theory group to other parallel stories (such as the black-ops monster-hunting unit from the blog *Observe and Terminate*) made their appearance. In all the tellings of the tale, Zero strikes a clearly effective, wounding blow against Slenderman... but is grievously wounded in return. He disappears, and is possibly dead.

In most senses, however – both in-game and OOG – the Solstice Event was not a success. In-game, the Core Theory bloggers continued to be pursued and attacked. Many of the participants – Zero himself, Robert Sagel and many others – are either horribly wounded, killed or turned into Proxies. Although attempts are made after that point to use the Tulpa Effect again, none seem to cause any lasting harm to Slenderman or his minions.

Out-of-game, Core Theory, though popular, was also highly criticised. Many bloggers felt that the whole Core Theory concept reduced the power of the mythos as horror – because something that can be successfully fought just isn't as scary. Others insisted that the addition of archetypally-bestowed abilities to the mythos was leading to a wave of blogs which were nothing more than super-hero tales, with the protagonists functioning simply as Mary Sues (wish-fulfilment personifications of the writer). Even some of the Core Theory writers themselves – including Gratt and the creator of Zero – agreed with this OOG, and later wrote other stories to retroactively change the continuity of their stories ('retcon') so that the powers weren't as effective or useful, to counteract this trend.

From a writer and horror fan's perspective, I see their point. But at the same time, as someone looking at the Slenderman phenomenon from the perspective of a practicing modern magician with considerable experience in working with avowedly fictional entities, the thought which kept going round and round my head when reading of Sagel and Zero et al's noble battle against this awful foe, was: "If only they'd read more comic books..."

Specifically, the comics of Alan Moore and Grant Morrison.

## Idea-Space and the Hypersigil

"Ideas are bullet proof."
– Codename V, in Alan Moore's *V for Vendetta*

"I'm an assassin – I can kill anything."
– King Mob, in Grant Morrison's *The Invisibles*

Alan Moore and Grant Morrison are two of the most important, and generally underestimated, cultural influences of the late 20th and early 21st centuries. That's no hyperbole – if you just consider the impact of Anonymous (symbolized by the Guy Fawkes mask from Moore's *V For Vendetta*) and the film *The Matrix* (which was strongly influenced by, or possibly part-plagiarized from, Morrison's epic *The Invisibles*, of which more below), their thought has filtered into modern culture with lasting effect.

Although they are (infamously) far from friends, they have much in common. Both are British (Moore from the town of Northampton in the north of England, Morrison from Glasgow, Scotland). Both were born into the working class. Both have produced classic works in the comic book mainstream which changed the industry greatly, but also have worked outside the Big Two of DC and Marvel Comics.

And…both are practicing magicians, who have each had powerful personal experiences of the fictional bursting into the supposedly Real World. Each of them has a theory about just how that can be – and both these theories bring an important perspective to the Slenderman phenomenon.

Alan Moore

Alan Moore's experience with magic grew from the vast amount of research he conducted for his various works, from as far back as his ground-breaking run on DC Comics' *Swamp Thing*, in which he created the character of John Constantine. Constantine, a sarcastic, morally ambiguous working-class Englishman with a strong resemblance to Sting and a notable lack of respect for the niceties of both ceremonial magic and supposed authority, became a break-out character, featuring in his own long-running comic *Hellblazer*. In its unbroken 24-year run, *Hellblazer* has been written by the very cream of modern comic writers – creators such as Neil Gaiman, Garth Ennis, Warren Ellis, Mike Carey, Peter Milligan…and Grant Morrison.

Although Moore's own career took him away from writing Constantine after his initial *Swamp Thing* run – as he came to fame for such works as *Watchmen*, *V For Vendetta*, *Batman: The Killing Joke* and his epic, occult-and-psychogeography-drenched Jack The Ripper opus *From Hell* – the character continued to linger in his mind…to the point where Moore has publicly admitted to encountering John Constantine in the real world. Twice.

Moore told of his first encounter with Constantine in the flesh to *Wizard Magazine* (which, it should be noted, was a comic industry work, not an occult zine!) thus:

> One day, I was in Westminster in London – this was after we had introduced the character - and I was sitting in a sandwich bar. All of a sudden, up the stairs came John Constantine. He was wearing the trenchcoat, a short cut, he looked…no, he didn't even look exactly like Sting. He looked exactly like John Constantine. He looked at me, stared me straight in the eyes, smiled, nodded almost conspiratorially, and then just walked off around the corner to the other part of the snack bar.
>
> I sat there and thought, should I go around that corner and see if he is really there, or should I just eat my sandwich and leave? I opted for the latter; I thought it was the safest. I'm not making any claims to anything. I'm just saying that it happened. Strange little story.

His second meeting with John Constantine is recounted as part of his theatrical performance piece, *Snakes and Ladders* (which was adapted into comic form by the artist Eddie Campbell as *A Disease Of Language* – in direct reference to the earlier Crowley quote):

> Years later, in another place, he steps out of the dark and speaks to me. He whispers: "I'll tell you the ultimate secret of magic. Any c*nt could do it."

In a personal conversation with me in 2011, Moore said that this encounter took place in the context of a magical ritual. But under the circumstances, that may make it more relevant here, rather than less.

At the age of 40, partly as a result of the deep assimilation of occult lore required to write *From Hell*, Moore publicly announced that he was now a magician. Furthermore, he added that his specific focus of worship was the little-known ancient Greek deity Glycon – a snake-god which, by most accounts, was actually nothing more than a glove puppet operated by a fraudulent priest. Clearly, Moore's take on magic was not to be limited to the traditional forms of ritual worship and was able to embrace the validity of fictional forms as a magical focus, as first proposed by the practitioners of what would eventually be called Chaos Magic.

His magical praxis brought a deeper structure to his later works, especially in his mammoth retelling of the Western esoteric tradition in comic form, *Promethea* (featuring another god-figure created entirely from human imagination) and in his ongoing potpourri of fictional worlds *The League of Extraordinary Gentlemen*. In the latter, Moore advances his theory of how the imaginal and physical realms may interact – a concept he has named 'Idea-space'.

Essentially, Moore's concept of Idea-space is that there is a parallel level of reality to ours which is both inhabited by, and the source of, every idea humans have or ever will have. That the concepts and characters we think we create are actually discovered. As Moore puts it:

> Maybe our individual and private consciousness is, in Idea-space terms, the equivalent of owning an individual and private house, an address, in material space? The space inside our homes is entirely ours, and yet if we step out through the front door, we find ourselves in a street, a world, that is mutually accessible and open to anyone. What if that was true of the mind, as well? What if it were possible to travel beyond the confines of one's individual mind-space, into the communal outdoors, where one could meet with the minds of other people in a shared place? This would at a stroke explain dubious phenomena such as reported telepathy or knowledge-at-a-distance. When James Watt discovered steam propulsion, for example, there were a number of other inventors who came up with the idea independently in that same year, yet were unable to beat Watt to the Patent Office... If Idea-space doesn't exist, then these numerous independent discoveries of steam power can only be an almost unbelievable coincidence.

This conception of a realm in which human consciousness can overlap with 'fictional' forms clearly has relevance for the concept of thought-forms in general, and the Slenderman phenomenon in particular.

Grant Morrison's experience with magic is rather different to Moore's. Morrison was practicing magic from the relatively early age of 17, thanks to an uncle who lent him various works by Aleister Crowley. His success with these rituals, combined with his taste for the outlandish public personas in rock and punk music (as well as a deep admiration for Michael Moorcock's dandyish character Jerry Cornelius, The English Assassin) led Morrison to increasingly combine his magic, writing and personal life. He, like Moore, shot to fame as a result of being recruited by DC Comics as part of the British Wave of writers intended to invigorate the industry in the 1980s. Right from the first, in his reboot of the obscure C-list superhero *Animal Man*, Morrison's work was looking hard at the metatextural...to the extent that, when he finished his run on the book, the last issue had the hero meet a version *of Morrison himself* as a creator-figure – in this instance, of Morrison apologising for the travails he had put the character through for the sake of a good story.

Grant Morrison

Morrison's interest in surrealism and the edgier realms of philosophy and the occult were increasingly instrumental in his work – coming to the fore in books such as his version of *Doom Patrol* and his breakthrough Batman story *Arkham Asylum*. His success was such that the editors of DC's adult-oriented Vertigo Comics imprint were willing to take a risk on an original comic series from Morrison, one which would make a huge mark on comics in general, and Morrison himself in particular – a series called *The Invisibles*.

It was to be the tale of the modern descendants of The Invisible College – the age-old magically-enhanced anarchist conspiracy who battled to hold in check the forces of authoritarianism. And, it was, from the first, intended to heavily reflect Morrison's experience with chaos magic – especially the sigil tool set derived from the early 20$^{th}$ century practitioner and artist Austin Osman Spare.

As Morrison explains it in his chaos magic tutorial *Pop Magic!*:

> The sigil takes a magical desire or intent – let's say "IT IS MY DESIRE TO BE A GREAT ACTOR" (you can, of course, put any desire you want in there) and folds it down, creating a highly-charged symbol. The desire is then forgotten. Only the symbol remains and can then be charged to full potency when the magician chooses. Forgetting the desire in its verbal form can be difficult if you've started too ambitiously. There is no point charging a sigil to win the lottery if you don't buy a ticket.

...I've also used sigils for healing, for locating lost objects and for mass global change. I've been using them for 20 years and they ALWAYS work. For me the period between launching the sigil and its manifestation as a real world event is usually 3 days, 3 weeks, or 3 months depending on the variables involved. I repeat: sigils ALWAYS work.

So. Begin your desire's transformation into pure throbbing symbol in the following fashion: First remove the vowels and the repeating letters to leave a string of consonants – TSMYDRBGC. Now start squashing the string down, throwing out or combining lines and playing with the letters until only an appropriately witchy-looking glyph is left.

...There are no rules as to how your sigil should look as long as it WORKS for you. RESULTS ONLY are important at this stage. If something doesn't work, try something else. The point is not to BELIEVE in magic, the point is to DO it and see how it works. This is not religion and blind faith plays no part.

Charging and launching your sigil is the fun part...

Morrison then notes that a sigil is to be charged by a powerful, focussed release of emotional energy. Any stimulus can be used – a common one is masturbation, the sigil to be concentrated on, visualized and empowered at the moment of orgasm.

In *The Invisibles*, Morrison wanted to expand the concept of sigil magic beyond the limits of the single image – it was to be, in the term he coined, a *hypersigil*. As he defined it, "The hypersigil is a sigil extended through the fourth dimension."

The entirety of *The Invisibles* – every line of dialogue, every drawn frame – would be an aspect of a huge spell to alter reality at a fundamental level. Morrison's intent was to awaken a higher level of magical consciousness in the world as a way of allowing people to greater control their lives in the face of increasingly authoritarian times – and to alter his own life on a deep level, to re-imagine himself into a better man. To this end, he used many aspects of his own life story in the text, especially in the creation of a character designed to be the archetypal version of who and what he wanted to become: King Mob.

The book had an enthusiastic, but small, audience when it was first published in 1994. Aspects of the book soon began to show powerful recursive effects in Morrison's life; to an extent, he was starting to become King Mob. This, however, had its drawbacks.

Towards the end of the first run of *The Invisibles*, King Mob is captured by the forces of Order, and brutally tortured. One part of the torture involved his being convinced that the enemy had mutilated his face with a necrotizing fasciitis virus, leaving a huge disfiguring hole in his cheek. As those issues of the book reached print, Morrison fell grievously ill, nearly dying. One of the symptoms was an infection which made a hole in his cheek.

When Morrison recovered, he sensibly decided to alter King Mob's character trajectory into something which would be less damaging in terms of magical backlash. He was further informed by the visions he had in his near-death experience, changing the storyline of *The Invisibles* to a more optimistic outcome and influencing powerful later works such as *The Filth*, *All-Star Superman* and *Batman RIP*. His interest in magic has never wavered.

(He also published a sigil in the letters page of the end of *The Invisibles*' first volume, designed to raise sales of the book…and to be charged with the orgasmic power of the readers. This act, known as The Wank-a-thon, is now legendary…especially as sales of the book increased dramatically, allowing the series to reach its natural, er, conclusion five years later.)

All of which is a roundabout way of allowing me to ask the following: What if the entirety of the Slenderman mythos, this brutal intrusion from Idea-space, is an accidental hypersigil?

## Hacking the Hypersigil

"You made it real! You can make it unreal."
- Emily Jessup, in Paddy Chayefsky's *Altered States*

It is, of course, entirely possible that the people mentioned at the start of this article who phoned in to Coast To Coast AM were simply lying. Playing the Slenderman ARG, planting the idea of his reality into a paranormal talk show just for the lulz. But, on one level, that doesn't actually matter. Stories like this feed into the overall myth structure of Slenderman, act to enhance the hypersigil, more deeply delineate into (or, perhaps, reinvest from) his Idea-space form. Right from the start, in the *Something Awful* thread mere days after Victor Surge's original pair of photoshopped pictures began the whole thing, the commenter known as 'T' said:

> The Slender Man.
> He exists because you thought of him.
> Now try and not think of him.

We can't. The same as the old saying about hearing the words White Elephant and trying not to imagine a white elephant – or, for those who've read so far, the blog *White Elephants*. So, in one sense, we can't kill Slenderman. We made him real.

But, as the quote from *Altered States* above notes: we can make him unreal. In the same way the Core Theory group tried (but failed), in the way Grant Morrison did successfully with King Mob – we can edit the story. Magic is, after all, a disease of language – a ghost haunting the space between reality and the symbols we use to describe reality – which are all we can ever truly know of reality.

We can manipulate the symbol-set.
We can hack the hypersigil.
And we can certainly take action against any single instance of him. Any c*nt could do it.

One of the most powerful principles in the array of techniques that have become known as Chaos magic is banishing with laughter. Most often used at the end of a ritual to disrupt and free any lingering magical energies (and as a clear crossing-point back to 'reality' from magical space), it's most often applied as sharing a good, hearty group laugh. But it can also be used as a weapon.

The power of ridicule and satire against figures of authority is well-known. The powerful rarely appreciate being laughed at. And, it seems, Slenderman is no different. Many of the blogs diverge from the serious horror-show and creepypasta of the mythos and simply take the piss.

Born in a 2-minute video spoof and now distributed nearly as widely as Slenderman himself is his sweet-natured, fun-loving brother *Splendorman!* (the exclamation point is important). There are even stories where people have used the spirit of Splendorman! (pictured to the right) to successfully banish Slenderman.

Another effective set of spoofs used as anti-Slendy magic in-game revolve around another short parody video, which takes a *Marble Hornets* clip and adds to the soundtrack the (rather tedious) rap song "Gimme Twenty Dollars" by Roy Browz. It's catchy and annoying – and at least one member of the initial Core Theory Group (Madurin the Jester of *A Really Bad Joke*) managed to actually banish an instance of Slenderman by handing him a $20 bill.

If Slenderman were to make actual inroads into quotidian reality, I think it's tools like these that would best oppose him. Fighting fire – to quote the film *Toys* – with marshmallows.

And let's be clear – a full formed manifestation of Slenderman is pretty damn unlikely. Chaos mages have been trying to manifest Great Cthulhu in ritual for decades since Kenneth Grant popularized H.P. Lovecraft's work in his magical theories, and the world remains uneaten. But he could – and may – haunt the edges of our consciousness, pull us in to notable synchronicities. Manifest as thoroughly-yet-tenuously as John Constantine did to Alan Moore, become as significant as King Mob was to Grant Morrison.

In that event, we have to remember that, whatever else Slenderman may be, he is a *creation*, a story, a trick of the mind. And, if I may leave you with one more quote – this time from the modern Holy Fool Pee-Wee Herman…

Your mind plays tricks on you? You play tricks back!

**Ian 'Cat' Vincent** was born on Imbolc-Groundhog Day in Gravesend, England, 1964. He is a lifelong student of the occult, and a former professional combat magician, curse-breaker and exorcist. In recent years, he has focused on exploring the utility of the 'hyper-real' (fiction-inspired) belief systems. His writing on Forteana and magic, especially on the personal magical style he terms 'Guttershaman', can be found at http://catvincent.com. He is also a staff writer at http://weaponizer.co.uk and http://modernmythology.net and co-curates the consciousness news/ discussion group http://fuckyeahconsciousness.tumblr.com. He lives in Yorkshire, England with his wife, the artist and writer Kirsty Hall. He is often found on Twitter as @catvincent.

He's a nasty piece of work. Just ask anyone.

# The Enigmatic Doctor Dee

## Scientist. Scholar. Spy.
## (And Talked With Angels)

by *Robert M. Schoch, Ph.D.*

John Dee, the great English magus, bibliophile, scholar, mathematician, astronomer, astrologer, occultist, and advisor to Queen Elizabeth, was characterized by a seeming inconsistency, an almost schizoid syndrome, on the surface. Born in Mortlake, a village on the Thames outside of London, 13 July 1527,[1] Dee's father was either a vintner and/or a tailor to King Henry VIII. Dee studied Latin and entered St. John's College, Cambridge, in 1542. There he claimed to have studied eighteen hours a day, taking breaks only for religious observances. He graduated and became a fellow of St. John's, and in December 1546 was appointed an under-reader of Greek at Trinity College. In May 1547 he made his first trip to continental Europe, attending the

University of Louvain (Belgium) where he developed a friendship with the great geographer Gerardus Mercator. Dee returned to England to take an M.A. degree at Cambridge, then spent the summer of 1548 through July 1550 on the continent – studying at Louvain and lecturing at the University of Paris. Although commonly referred to as "Doctor Dee" even during his lifetime,[2] there is currently no solid evidence that he ever formally was awarded a doctorate by any university. He may have simply been addressed as "Doctor" in recognition of his universally acknowledged vast learning, although it has been suggested that Dee may have been awarded a doctorate in medicine by the University of Prague.[3]

In 1551 Dee first became deeply involved with the English Court, coming under the patronage of Sir William Cecil (1521 – 1598) who at that time was Secretary of State to Edward VI, and would serve in various capacities to the monarchs Edward VI, Jane Grey, Mary, and Elizabeth. As described further below, Dee was not always in good graces with the Court – he was imprisoned for a short time in 1555 – but with the accession of Elizabeth as Queen (reigned 1558 – 1601), he appears to have been favored for the majority of the rest of his life. Indeed, Elizabeth was quite fond of Dee, consulting him on many important matters. Dee not only astrologically advised her on the best day for her coronation, but he also sent intelligence back to her during his trips through Europe. In other words, Dee may have been Elizabeth's secret agent.[4]

During the 1560s through 1580s Dee, along with his family and household, split his time between traveling through continental Europe and living in Great Britain. It was during the period of about 1581 through 1589 that he was most extensively involved in his now infamous séances, his angelic conversations, with various scryers or mediums, but most notably Edward Kelley. Many of these sessions took place while on the move in continental Europe. On 2 December 1589 Dee returned to England, after a six-year absence, and lived out the last two decades of his life, dying in December 1608 (or possibly early in 1609). At the end of his life Dee was described as having "a very faire cleare rosie complexion, a long beard as white as milke; he was tall and slender; a very handsome...mighty good man he was... He wore a Gowne like an Artist's, with hanging sleeves, and a slitt."[5] In his prime Dee was not only a highly learned scholar and magus but also a robust specimen of a man, known to be a good horseman, a fancier of steeple-chases, a keeper of hounds, and a sponsor of lavish parties that included dancing and fireworks.[6]

Doctor John Dee by most superficial accounts and glosses was an honest, good, naively innocent, pious, and godly man of devout Christian faith, who would in the end utilize methods of scrying (in particular, crystal gazing with the assistance of a medium) as a way to converse with God's angels in an attempt to gain superhuman knowledge and omniscience. In the words of Dee scholar György E. Szőnyi, "the English Doctor did not make a covenant with the Devil".[7] However, I believe the evidence leads us to the opposite conclusion. Dee, I suspect, possessed genuine paranormal powers, and his "angels" where certainly not imaginary (even if they were arguably of his own making, the knowledge they brought had in some but not all cases a veridical basis). But were they "angels" as Dee wanted to believe, or "devils"? Dee may have deluded himself and made a Faustian-style pact with lesser darker spirits, a pact sealed with sexual-magical rites of a traditional "black magic" nature that ostensibly Dee abhorred and repudiated. Common threads throughout Dee's research and life are an obsession with knowledge (and thus power and prestige), and he was even willing to commit adultery at the promise of gaining knowledge. Dee's quest for ultimate knowledge and godlike understanding is evident both in his perhaps most famous publication, the *Monas Hieroglyphica* (1564) and his angelic conversations (Enochian magic). I will consider each in turn, but first we need to mention a work that inspired Dee.

## Steganographia (Secret Writing)

Perhaps one of the most profound influences on Dee's subsequent research, career, and personal life was the discovery, while traveling in the Low Countries in late 1562 or early 1563, of a manuscript copy of *Steganographia* ('Secret Writing') by Johannes Trithemius (1462 – 1516). This was possibly made known to Dee on his visit to Antwerp through the typographer and bookseller Christopher Plantin[8] or by the Dutch printer Willem Silvius in whose home Dee stayed.[9] Trithemius was for twenty-two years an abbot at the Benedictine abbey of Sponheim, resigning in 1505, only to join the Benedictine cloister of Wurzburg a year later.[10] Trithemius was extremely well read and wrote extensively; *Steganographia* was completed by about 1500,[11] and had limited circulation in manuscript form for over a hundred years before its first print publication in 1606.[12] Dee was lent a manuscript of the book and spent ten solid days copying half of it, and an (unnamed) Hungarian nobleman copied the rest for him.[13] Writing on 16 February 1563 to Sir William Cecil back in England, Dee stated he had found a book, "the most precious juell that I have yet of other mens travailes recovered",[14] "a boke for which many a lerned man has long sought and dayly doth seeke; *whose use is greater than the fame thereof is spread*. The title is on this wise 'Stegan[o]graphia Joannes Tritemij'."[15]

*Steganographia* was, purposefully on many levels, a secretive book. It was regarded by a number of Trithemius's and Dee's contemporaries (as well as subsequent readers, right up into modern times) as a powerful manual of daemonic magic, and thus heretical despite being penned by a learned and respected abbot. This is not surprising, in that it records the names of numerous daemons (angels, spirits, and devils) along with the invocations to be used in summoning them. While some in modern times[16] have interpreted the *Steganographia* as primarily or solely a treatise on cryptography,[17] the truth seems to be more complex. *Steganographia* was not only a work on cryptography, encipherment, and secret writing; it was also a book of applied magic, including alchemy, cabbalistic number symbolism, demonology, angelology, occult philosophy, and other types of esoteric studies. If Trithemius was accused or suspected of any one of these subjects, his fall back position could be that his book was actually on one of the other subjects. But, in fact, it treated all of these subjects seriously. Indeed, one aspect of the work was the transmission of thoughts from one person to another over great distances without words, writing, or signs – that is, what we would now label telepathic transmission.[18] This, arguably, is the underlying basis of all scrying, séances, and various forms of "fortune telling", and includes telepathic transmissions not only geographically (from one place to another) but also temporally (both forward into the future and back into the past).[19]

The discovery of a copy of *Steganographia* appears to have crystallized many of Dee's thoughts and studies that had been incubating for years, even decades. The immediate result was his *Monas Hieroglyphica*. Later, still inspired by the work of Trithemius, Dee would undertake his conversations with 'angels'.

## The Meaning of the Hieroglyphic Monad

The work of which Dee was most proud, and for which he is famous (along with his angelic conversations), is the *Monas Hieroglyphica*, a short book that Dee composed over twelve days in January 1564 (although he had been working on the topic for years) and which was published in Antwerp in March 1564.[20] In this Hermetic treatise, consisting of twenty-four theorems based on and describing a symbol known as the hieroglyphic monad (as illustrated on the title page of his monograph), Dee attempted to embody universal knowledge that would, he believed, be destined to revolutionize the arts and sciences.[21] Ultimately, its exact meaning and significance – both what Dee intended, and what is encoded occultly in the monad –

Title page of *Monas Hieroglyphica*, 1564.

is subject to debate. For Dee, the monad was a "cosmic image"[22] that served many functions, including as a symbol or talisman of potent power and a sort of "revelatory mandala" for introspective contemplation and "an intuitive understanding of the cosmos and a unification with the wisdom of God."[23] To properly understand the *Monas Hieroglyphica* one needed private instruction or a key; manuscript copies and word of mouth versions of such instruction may have circulated during Dee's lifetime and shortly thereafter, but now seem to be lost (unless secreted away by select initiates who will not reveal what they know). Dee personally explained his work to both Queen Elizabeth and Emperor Rudolf II (Rudolph II).[24]

Dee's monad was based on ancient precedents, though he presented it in a novel form. A common idea, one that has "characterized most times and cultures – an insight corroborated by anthropology", is "that intellectual progress depends on the recovery of knowledge attained by the ancients."[25]

> According to Dee, ancient magi had known the true structure of the heavens and preserved their knowledge for subsequent generations in the common planetary signs that they carefully designed not only to represent the heavenly bodies but also to reveal cryptically what was true about them.[26]

This he took advantage of in designing the hieroglyphic monad, and in his explanations of it. It is not known precisely when Dee first hit upon the design of the hieroglyphic monad, but he used it on the title page of his 1558 book, *Propaedeumata Aphoristica* ('An Aphoristic Introduction'), consisting of 120 aphorisms dealing with the connections between astronomy, geometry, and astrology,[27] although Dee did not explicitly discuss the monad in his 1558 book.

Superficially Dee's hieroglyphic monad looks like the standard astronomical symbol for Mercury combined with the symbol for Aries at its base. However, there are subtle differences: in the original hieroglyphic monad the upper crescent does not rest on the circle, but interlinks with it, and the circle has a center. This signifies, as Dee states explicitly in Theorem X of the *Monas Hieroglyphica*, that the basic elements of the hieroglyphic monad are the Moon (crescent), Sun (circle with central point indicated), the cross representing the four basic elements and the terrestrial realm, and the astrological sign of Aries (representing alchemically the fire or the heat necessary for transmutation).[28] The four elements, in a material sense, were traditionally water, earth, fire, and air[29] or moisture, cold, heat, and dryness,[30] but for Dee they were also "to be, to live, to feel and to comprehend (*esse, vivere, sentire et entelligere*)."[31]

The exact origin of the hieroglyphic monad is unclear; Dee implied that he had designed it himself when he complained, in a handwritten note preserved on his personal copy of *Chymisticum Artificium Naturae* (1568) that the author of that work, Gerard Dorn, had reproduced a version of the hieroglyphic monad without so much as acknowledging Dee.[32] Szőnyi suggested that in a general sense the monad may have been inspired by and derived from the ancient use of circles and crosses.[33] Dee, according to Szőnyi, read about their symbolic significance in the works of the Neo-Platonist Marsilio Ficino (1433 – 1499) which he possessed and studied, and from that discussion derived his monad.[34] I will take Szőnyi's hypothesis further

The ancient symbol of an equilateral cross within a circle, seen here on a late 6th century BCE silver coin from Athens, Greece.

and suggest that Dee derived his monad from arguably one of the most ancient and fundamental symbols or talismans, that of an equilateral cross, surmounted by a point at the intersection of the arms of the cross, within a circle (and on the most refined versions of this symbol, four ever so slight quarter crescents are indicated on the inner portions of the circle between the points where the arms of the cross join the circle). This symbol has been viewed as a primordial solar symbol, the wheel of the Sun (and the later symbol for the Sun is a circle with a central point, as already noted), and also the symbol for planet Earth (the circle containing the cross, representing as well the four cardinal points). Indeed it combines both. Sometimes, particularly among classicists, it is simply referred to as a "chariot wheel" and this symbol appears in the context of chariots and other vehicles in Greek and Roman times, but it is also the wheel of fortune, the wheel of the movement of the heavens, the reflection of the connection between the celestial and terrestrial ("as above, so below"), the divine and the mundane, and much more. Dee's hieroglyphic monad separates the circle and point from the cross, placing them on top of the cross. Of the crescents, it places a half-circle crescent at the very top interlocking with the circle, and it places the remaining two smaller crescents (call them quarter crescents) at the base of the cross, forming the symbol of the fire or Aries.

The hieroglyphic monad, and Dee's writings and teachings about it, was (it seems) intended to reveal all essential astronomical and alchemical knowledge, cabbalistic intelligence, the basis of all geometry and mathematical knowledge, the structure of the cosmos (both the macrocosm and the microcosm), and the nature of the human condition. Furthermore, from the hieroglyphic monad could be generated all numbers and all of the alphabets of all languages including, most importantly, the first language of Adam (and of God), the *lingua adamica* (also referred to as the Enochian language, which Dee would later seek knowledge of through the angelic conversations). The *lingua adamica* was of extreme importance because in this first and primordial language of God could be found not just knowledge but also power in the words. Indeed, the monad itself, if its use was properly understood, was a powerful magic talisman. By harnessing the talismanic powers of the monad, the Magus could[35] command spirits, perform alchemical transmutations, and finally and most importantly undergo the "mystical transmutation of 'understanding,' the *exaltatio*"[36] and, I would add, harness what in modern parlance might be called paranormal powers to effect real changes in the world we know.[37]

Such lofty and mystical goals set forth in the *Monas Hieroglyphica* do not preclude more pragmatic uses of the monad and accompanying treatise, both in terms of conjuring and in terms of encoding ciphers for secret messages, such as for espionage purposes. There are many reasons to believe that Dee acted, at least in part, as a spy for Queen Elizabeth. Dee even used the code name 007 (apparently representing Dee's eyes serving the queen, with a bar over the eyes and a line to the right – plus seven is a sacred number, a number of mystery and divinity); 007 was later adopted by Ian Fleming for his James Bond character.[38] But without Dee's personal teaching or unpublished key to the *Monas Hieroglyphica* these aspects of the treatise are highly elusive, to say the least.

## THE MONAD AND LEVI'S BAPHOMET

Here I wish to point out what, to me, are some obvious similarities between Dee's hieroglyphic monad and the "Sabbatic Goat" or "Baphomet of Mendes", particularly as reconstructed in the now famous nineteenth century depiction by Éliphas Lévi (presumably based on much earlier Templar prototypes combined with Hermetic, alchemical, and cabbalistic symbology – the originals being deeply guarded secrets and thus not available to profane eyes[39]). Superficially, at first glance, it may seem like a stretch to seriously compare Dee's monad with Lévi's Baphomet, but pursuing it further, I do believe there are real connections. Lévi's Baphomet can be derived or deduced from the monad, and vice versa: ultimately, at a fundamental level, they may represent the same principles, although taking different external forms. Athanasius Kircher in his *Oedipus Aegyptiacus* (1653 – 1658) reproduced and discussed Dee's hieroglyphic monad (without citing Dee, however), and also put forth an elaborate "Mathematica Hieroglyph" based on Dee's monad, but added further decorative elements, such as turning the Aries symbol into a snake[40] which is not far from the caduceus of Lévi's Baphomet. Dee, in his learning, would certainly have been aware of various early forms of Baphomet (in written descriptions as well as depictions), from which Lévi ultimately derived his illustration. Lévi, in turn, took an interest in the work of Dee's associate Edward Kelley,[41] and therefore must have had some familiarity with the work of Dee and his most famous book, the *Monas Hieroglyphica*. As a side note, Aleister Crowley was greatly influenced by the angelic conversations and Enochian

The Baphomet as reconstructed by Éliphas Lévi (from *Dogme et Rituel de la Haute Magie* (second edition), vol. 2 (*Rituel*), frontispiece, 1861).

Magic of John Dee and Edward Kelley, reproducing and extending such practices, particularly by incorporating extensive sexual rites within the Dee-Kelley framework.[42] Crowley believed, or at least claimed, that he had been both Edward Kelley and Éliphas Lévi in previous incarnations.

Perhaps more to the point are the depiction, description, and discussion of Dee's monad in an important magical-alchemical synthesis written and published in Dee's lifetime: *Il Mondo Magico di gli Heroi* ('The Magical World of the Heroes') by Cesare della Riviera (1605), particularly as discussed by della Riviera's modern disciple and interpreter Julius Evola.[43] Although Evola acknowledged that the monad symbol is found in Dee (1564), della Riviera precisely reproduced and discussed the monad without ever mentioning Dee by name.[44] Was this a simple oversight? I suspect not. Rather, my hunch is that the monad had entered the consciousness of many hermeticists and magi, perhaps often through secret manuscript copies of the key that apparently pertained to the *Monas Hieroglyphica* (possibly without ever having seen an actual printed copy of the *Monas*) and there may have been a widespread attitude that the monad was a universal and eternal symbol that should not or need not be associated with any particular person. Certainly della Riviera was not the only writer to discuss the monad without citing Dee; others included Athanasius Kircher.[45]

Evola describes the monad, which he refers to as an ideogram, as a "synthesis of the condition of the human being" (which as a microcosm reflects the macrocosm):

> The vulgar Moon and Sun ([the crescent sign of the Moon with both horns pointed upward] and [the sign of the Sun, a circle with a dot in the center]) – that is the exteriorizations of ordinary waking consciousness – are in ascendance (above) with regard to the elemental forces of the Body (symbolized by the cross [the sign of the cross]), which, however, in their depths ([the

sign of Aries] in turn is found under [the sign of the cross]), are recapitulated by the primordial virile form, [the sign of Aries], the sign already explained as Θεῖον – Sulfur or Divine Energy – in a 'pure state'.[46]

Pursuing Evola's (based on della Riviera) description of the monad further, the similarities to Lévi's "hieroglyphic figure"[47] or Baphomet are remarkable. The Sun and Moon of the monad correspond to the head and its cerebral organ,[48] the equivalent of the head of Baphomet with the horns (Moon) and torch of "equilibrating intelligence",[49] and the pentagram on the forehead with one point in the ascendant representing the microcosm and revelation.[50] The cross of the monad corresponds to the body or "middle zone of the human organism with the center in the heart, which is equivalent to the center of said cross and thence to Quintessence, to the secret Heaven, the Water of Life, and all the other symbols referring to the 'Spirit' principle".[51] This is the body proper, the arms, and the wings of the illustration of Baphomet, which in turn are further elaborated symbols of the spirit, its attributes, its workings, its dualities and subdivisions, and ultimately its secrets of unity and redemption. On the arms of Lévi's Baphomet are inscribed "*Solve [et] Coagula*" (dissolve or solution or breaking down, and coagulation or coming together), referring to the alchemical work of breaking down, reworking, and transmutation, whether it be of base metal to create gold in a physical sense, or more generally causing transformations in the outer world, body, mind, consciousness, spirit, or psyche – harnessing the power of natural and occult forces and agents to effect change, and most importantly inner change, the essence of the Great Work. Indeed, Lévi explicitly notes that the figure of Baphomet represents the Great Work.[52] As Evola writes, referring to the monad (but his words apply equally well to the "idol" Baphomet), "The contents of this region are essentially made up of *translations* of processes that at first are produced nonmaterially in the mid-region, manifesting forces still deeper".[53]

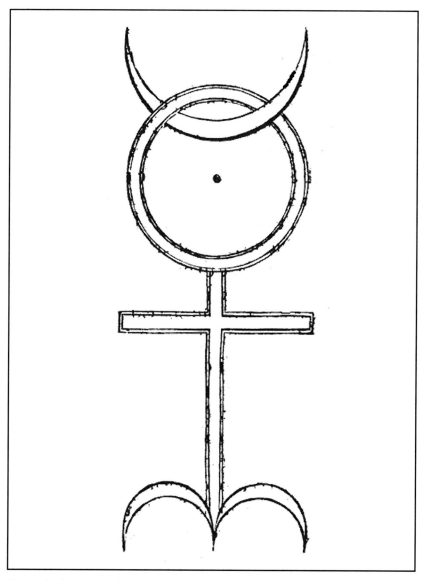

Hieroglyphic Monad as reproduced in della Riviera, 1605, page 24. Note that in della Riviera's version of the monad the arm on the left side of the top crescent goes under the circle, whereas it is the arm on the right side that does so on Dee's original. This may simply be a function of the artist directly copying Dee's original (or a copy of Dee's monad) when making the plate to be printed from, and thus the monad was reversed in printing.

Describing his image of Baphomet, Lévi wrote, "The lower portion of the body is veiled, portraying the mysteries of universal generation, which is expressed solely by the symbol of the caduceus."[54] Describing the equivalent portion of the monad, Evola writes:

> From the center of the Cross, which is the equivalent of the central and immobile hub out of which the 'wheel of the elements' rolls, we rejoin the third region, the inferior region corresponding to [the symbol of Aries]. This is the site of the nonhuman creative forces that in the corporeal structure crop up from the power of sexual generation, whose organs are situated precisely in the center of that which physically corresponds to this region. It is the foundation, the first root out of which everything springs into action through elemental processes to be manifested in the energies and internal and external forms of the particularized consciousness of the individual.[55]

Evola's comments apply equally well (if not better) to Baphomet! All in all, I hope that you, the reader, will seriously consider the possibility that Dee's hieroglyphic monad and Lévi's hieroglyphic figure of Baphomet are simply two versions of the same basic symbol and concept, a symbol that in and of itself is reflective of realities and possibilities and interconnections in the Cosmos, both the microcosm and macrocosm, but is neither "good" nor "bad". The Baphomet (and likewise the monad) is not inherently evil or a symbol of the "devil" except as some persons might want to brand or interpret it as such.

## Angel Conversations and Enochian Magic

Although Dee certainly did not conceal his conversations with angels, in his lifetime he did not widely publish on them either and they were not commonly known until a half century after his death when, in 1659, Meric Casaubon published portions of Dee's magical journals describing various scrying sessions along with other notes.[56] Casaubon's book formed the foundational basis for subsequent Enochian magic.[57] It has been suggested that Dee's interest in acquiring personal 'angel guides' may date back to a 1552 meeting with Gerolamo Cardano (1501 – 1576), a physician, scientist, astrologer, and practicing occultist who claimed to be guided by his own spirit, not unlike the daemon of Socrates.[58] According to his diaries, Dee began his studies in scrying no later than 1579, and possibly even as early as 1569.[59] They did not really take off, however, until he began to use Edward Kelley as his scryer and medium in 1582 – a close collaboration that would last until 1589. Ultimately Dee and Kelley developed an elaborate set of procedures for conversing with 'angels' that were primarily perceived (seen and heard) by Kelley who, using a crystal or "shew stone" (that is, via crystallomancy, considered a branch of "opticall science" in Dee's time[60]), would relate the details to Dee, acting as scribe. At times séances consisted of only Dee and Kelley, at other times various observers and guests were included.

The angels themselves were not physical entities. Rather, this is how Dee described them: "I do think you have no organs or Instruments apt for voyce, but are mere spirituall and nothing corporall, but have the power and property from God to insinuate your message or meaning to ear or eye so that man's imagination shall be that they hear and see you sensibly."[61] Through the 'angels', Dee hoped to learn the sought after *lingua adamica* or Enochian alphabet and language (named after the Old Testament character of Enoch, to whom God had previously revealed this primordial language), along with the basis of so-called Enochian magic. Dee, via the angels, desired to seek the direct company of the Deity and regain the *prisca theologia* ("the primitive wisdom of our ancestors"[62] or the original true ancient theology) that had been lost since the fall of humankind in Eden.

Needless to say, the entire issue of the validity (if any) of Dee's scrying adventures and conversations with angels has been a subject of heated controversy ever since. Conventional historians of science have tended to dismiss this phase of Dee's career as so much nonsense, while on the other hand certain occultists have taken the concept of Enochian magic very seriously, even putting it into practice with, in some cases, very tangible results (Aleister Crowley is but one example[63]). On the surface, Dee accepted that the angels were messengers from God, rather than from Satan/Lucifer and the darker forces. Yet there is evidence from the angels themselves that they were hardly pure and lovely, but often a bit peevish to downright perverse. Furthermore, they did not always give veridical information.

On numerous occasions Kelley charged that the 'angels' (the supposed spiritual beings they were communicating with) were wicked and evil, and at times Kelley wanted nothing more to do with them. Furthermore, they were far from omniscient, and not only in making prognostications that never came true, but seemingly lacking basic knowledge in some cases. Here are some examples. Concerning Albert Łaski (a Polish or Bohemian nobleman who met Dee and Kelley in England in 1583, and traveled with them through central and eastern Europe), it was predicted that he would become King of Poland, yet this never occurred.[64] In one case the angels seemed to be ignorant of basic geography.[65] In another case, they made arithmetical errors.[66] And in addressing Stephen Báthory (1533 – 1586), King of Poland (1576 – 1586), they were guilty of a major faux pas when they referred to him as having risen from the ranks of an ordinary soldier, which was hardly the case given that he was a member of a distinguished aristocratic family, and prior to being elected King was the Prince of Transylvania.[67]

The angels did, however, also relay veridical information that arguably could not be known through the normal senses. For instance, Deacon noted, "It is easy now to dismiss as roguery or guesswork the fact that in their [Dee's and Kelley's] spiritual exercises

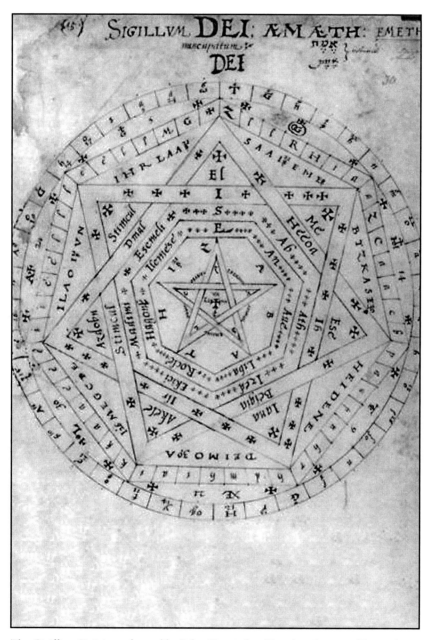

The *Sigillum Dei Aemeth*, used by John Dee in his 'Enochian' magic. The seal was imprinted on wax disks and used to protect the workings from outside influences.

they were able to verify lands that had not been properly charted, or point correctly to where gold could be found in the overseas possessions. The fact remains that such discoveries were afterwards acknowledged to be true, by men such as Hakluyt and Camden."[68] The angels made other predictions that appear to have been fulfilled, including the death of Mary, Queen of Scots, and the Spanish Armada.[69] In another case, an angel predicted that a certain person would be "devoured by fishes" within five months, and indeed he drowned at sea before that time was over.[70] Dee himself, and his second wife Jane Fromond, were both known to have prophetic and clairvoyant dreams, and also to have occasionally been plagued by poltergeist type phenomena, including rappings, knockings, and a fire that broke out mysteriously.[71]

The angels, as they imparted the Enochian alphabet and language, developed an elaborate cosmography of the universe, visible and invisible. They described how the Earth and the Air are partitioned and governed among angels, numbering ultimately in the tens of thousands.[72] Four Watchtowers stand at the four corners of Earth, with each Watchtower containing twelve gates that lead to "angelic 'cities' or dimensions of reality".[73] There are evocations (Calls or Keys) for summoning and commanding spirits and angels, and to open the "gates to the cities of wisdom."[74]

Interestingly, or one might say quite amazingly, even though Dee "could not have had access to the sacred text of the Book of Enoch" he seems "to have [had]…good informants [i.e., the "angels"] because Enoch's appearance in Dee's private mythology embedded in his angelic conversations shows interesting convergence with the since-discovered original Enochian literature".[75] For instance, Dee discusses "the chief Watchman" and the "Watch-Tower", which indeed are found in the Book of Enoch.[76]

Who, exactly, were the "angels"? Were they representatives of the Almighty Creator? Did they really have the ability to teach Dee the *lingua adamica*? Or were they of other stock? In one session, a spirit explicitly stated that the "angels" were not from God, as recorded in the following dialogue.

> SPIRIT: Are you so foolish to think that the power of God will descend into so base a place? . . . What greater imperfection than to imagine, much more believe, that the Angels of God will, or may descend into so filthie a place, as this corruptible stone is?
>
> DEE: What causeth thee to come here?
>
> SPIRIT: Thy folly.[77]

In an infamous series of sessions, toward the end of the partnership between Kelley and Dee, the impish spirit Madimi appeared lewdly naked, and reported that Dee and Kelley were required to share all things in common, including carnal knowledge of their wives – so-called "cross matching".[78] Dee proffered abhorrence to such acts, but gave in and after much discussion and misgivings on the part of the various participants, a written pact was drawn and signed by Dee, Kelley, and their wives; "the adulteries… [were] consummated on May 23, 1587".[79] This could be viewed as an alchemical (even homosexual) "marriage" between Dee and Kelley,[80] although in fact it spelled the beginning of the end of their relationship. What was in it for Dee? He, by his own admission, had "pawned" his soul[81] hoping, expecting, divine secrets to be subsequently revealed to him—in the words of Madimi, "That you may become full of understanding, and in knowledge above common men."[82] Dee does not appear to have ever been satisfied that this promise was fulfilled, casting doubt on the credibility and agenda of the 'angels'.

Donald Tyson, a modern practitioner of Enochian magic, has suggested a rather sinister agenda for the so-called angels with which Dee conversed, writing…

...it seems clear that it was the intention of the angels that the Keys be ritually applied to the Watchtowers, not so that human beings could learn divine secrets of nature, as Dee believed, but to open the way for the demons of Coronzon ["the Enochian name for Lucifer"[83]] to enter into our unconscious minds. Once firmly established in our personal unconscious, these spirits would then be able to gain an increasing control over our physical world by manipulating our perceptions, emotions and thoughts.[84]

Ultimately, according to this view, the intention of the 'angels' was to bring about the Apocalypse, a universal Armageddon. Has this now occurred, or will it in the future? I will leave this topic to be pondered by modern practitioners of Enochian rituals.

## Who, or What, was Edward Kelley?

Among Dee scholars, Edward Kelley (or Kelly) is almost universally considered a real, genuine, person, if not the most savory of characters. He is said to have been born on 1 August 1555 at Worcester, and some believe he attended Oxford using the alias Edward Talbot (or Talbott), the name by which he would first introduce himself to John Dee, but left Oxford after getting into some sort of trouble there.[85] He may have been trained as an apothecary[86] and he may have briefly been a secretary to the magus and occultist Thomas Allen.[87] Sometime around 1580 he was apparently convicted of some form of forgery, either falsifying title deeds and/or counterfeiting coins, and was pilloried and had his ears cut off or cropped; from then on he generally wore a black skullcap to hide the condition of his ears.[88] Kelley was also accused of necromancy and black magic, including the disinterring (with an accomplice) of a fresh corpse from a churchyard and using it to solicit predictions via an evil spirit concerning the "manner and time of the death of a Noble yong Gentleman."[89] Kelley is also reported to have indulged in various drugs, including aconite and nightshade, to artificially induce delirium and hallucinations,[90] a practice used by sixteenth-century witches.

Kelley, using the name Talbot, appeared at Dee's home in Mortlake on 10 March 1582,[91] applying for the job of medium or scryer. According to various accounts, Kelley also enticed Dee with a phial containing a red powder (supposedly the alchemical "powder of projection" that could turn base metal into gold) and an undeciphered alchemical manuscript that he claimed came from the ruins of Glastonbury (or possibly from Wales), that apparently included references to ten places in England/Britain containing hidden treasure.[92] Kelley became closely associated with Dee, acting as his scryer and associate in various alchemical and occult studies, living in his household, and traveling with Dee on the continent until they parted company in Bohemia (located in the modern Czech Republic) – Dee returning to England while Kelley remained behind under the patronage of Rudolf II. After Dee's departure, Kelley was knighted by the emperor for his alchemical work, but subsequently imprisoned in Prague when he would not or could not produce gold from meaner metals. He attempted an escape in November 1595, but fell from a wall, turret, or tower (some sort of battlement), broke his legs and sustained other injuries from which he died shortly thereafter.[93]

I noted that among Dee scholars, Kelley is *almost* universally considered a real, genuine, person. A notable exception is Roy Norvill who writes, in his book *The Language of the Gods* (1987), that "Edward Kelly [the spelling of the name that Norvill uses], as a real person, never existed, for he was nothing but an elaborate invention by Dee".[94] Norvill contends that Dee was an Hermetic initiate who purposefully and consistently wrote in allegory, both in his published works and in his private diaries and notes (which he realized other people would look through, and which were written with the possibility of potential publication). Dee purposefully portrayed himself as an immensely learned and erudite scholar who was also incredibly naïve and gullible, and thus taken advantage of by the younger and somewhat dishonest man, Edward Kelley, and the 'angels' that Kelley conjured up. As a side note, although it seems not to be the case that Dee was directly a founder of Rosicrucianism (an order linked with the more general Hermetic tradition), there appear to be strong correlations between Dee's travels and influence in central Europe and the rise of the Rosicrucians in the early seventeenth century.[95]

Norvill asserts that the name Edward Talbot is first mentioned in a diary entry by Dee on 9 March 1582, but the initials of Edward Kelley do not appear until 22 November 1582, and "there is no sound reason to identify one with the other".[96] By Norvill's hypothesis, various attributes of the fictitious Kelley serve sound allegorical purposes. That Kelley was convicted of falsifying deeds is a reflection of Dee falsifying the narrative (i.e., creating the fiction of Kelley and the angelic conversations). Kelley's conviction for counterfeiting coins refers to the alchemical transmutation of base metal to gold. The cutting off of Kelley's ears is an allegory of the loss of one's flesh, moving away from the physical and material, resulting ultimately in the transformation of the emphasis of one's consciousness to the inward and higher self and intelligence. The black skullcap is a symbol of the beginning of the mental process of the would-be adept, the long and difficult labor to control the will and master the forces of one's own mind while cleansing one's psyche of erroneous (if commonly accepted) ideas and assumptions. In this light, the angelic conversations and séances that Dee and Kelley supposedly carried out were simply a fiction created by Dee – "an elaborate allegorical joke", in the words of Norvill,[97] although I suspect that they masked something both more sinister (experiments and keys of genuine magic, daemonic magic, whether or not Kelley was real or perhaps a fill-in for numerous personages, real and fictitious) and more pragmatic (cryptographic codes, useful for espionage in particular), not unlike *Steganographia*.

Many other aspects of the supposed 'Edward Kelley' suggest, according to Norvill, that he never existed as a real life person. Kelley's notorious bad temper and fits would fit the concept of the would-be adept attempting to tame and control the mind and consciousness. I suggest that Kelley's delving into necromancy and apparent interest in wife-swapping and sexual rituals would provide a cover for Dee's own fascination with such practices. If the wife-swapping ("cross-matching") had really occurred, and the participants were really sworn to the utmost secrecy on pain of instant death,[98] then why did Dee record such actions in writing, taking the risk that they could be seen by prying eyes, or even be published? Concerning the red powder and alchemical manuscript that Kelley may have acquired from the ruins of Glastonbury, Dee himself visited Glastonbury in 1574[99] to study first-hand the ancient earthworks there that seem to represent the zodiac, and may contain the secret of the Magnum Opus (the Great Work). Indeed, I suggest that Dee allowed the fictitious Kelley to be the alchemist so as to avoid being charged with such activities.

This gets to the heart of why, according to Norvill, Dee would perpetuate such an elaborate and prolonged fiction. Dee had every reason to fear arrest and conviction, which could even carry a death sentence, for some form of sorcery, heresy, witchcraft, or the like. From an early age, Dee was occasionally accused (both formally and informally by rumor) of sorcery and black magic. The first time recorded may have been about 1546, when as part of staging a play by Aristophanes at Trinity College he created a mechanical "flying" beetle that was so realistic that some thought he must have used magic.[100] Much more seriously, in 1555 Dee was imprisoned for about three months on allegations of "lewde and vayne practices of calculating and conjuring",[101] apparently connected with his casting of horoscopes for Queen Mary (by invitation of the Queen) and her half sister, Princess Elizabeth (who later became Queen, and favored Dee); Dee's actual offense may have been to show Mary's horoscope to Elizabeth. He was charged with treason, and then heresy, but after some months regained his freedom. It may be significant to Dee's later care in concealing his activities with fictions, ruses, and false leads, that even while he was in prison a fellow cellmate, Barthlet Green, was burnt at the stake for heresy.[102] Such might be enough to make many a person a bit paranoid.

But what about contemporary accounts, independent of Dee, which seem to testify to the reality of Edward Kelley? Norvill[103] asserts that his fellow Hermeticists would have happily joined in on the fiction, including the Emperor Rudolf II who was deeply committed to Hermeticism, and thus would readily assent to allowing the fictional Kelley to carry the title of Knight of Bohemia (representing initiateship in Hermetic terms). Likewise, the books and tracts attributed to Kelley, and published under his name, were written by Dee (after all, it is not uncommon for authors to use pseudonyms, and Dee could easily have presented himself as Kelley's representative to those not in on the fiction). I would add that it is not impossible that aspects of the fictional Kelley may have been based on a real life Edward Kelley or Edward Talbot, but a person who never had the long, full, and odd life of the Edward Kelley of whom Dee writes. At the end of his life when Dee no longer had any use for Edward Kelley, he let him die in a manner befitting his allegorical existence. As often depicted on Card XVI of the Major Arcana of the Tarot, Kelley fell to his ultimate death from a tower or battlement, representing the death and release from the materialistic imprisonment of the mind and consciousness, following application of the Hermetic mental process combined with the experience of revelation.[104] Finally, Norvill argues that Kelley's very name points to his fictitious nature. Kelley, also spelled Kelly, and often spelled Kelle in Dee's original manuscripts, may be a form of word play (as so beloved by Dee, and Queen Elizabeth for that matter[105]). The French word for "what" is "quel" (pronounced "kel") and in the French of Dee's time it was spelled "quelle". This, according to Norvill, could represent the Hermetic phrase loosely translated as "What is it?", a clear giveaway that we are dealing with Hermetic allegory.[106]

If Norvill is correct about the non-existence of Edward Kelley, not only might the fiction have served as an elaborate allegorical joke and cover for Dee's Hermetic and heretical thinking, along with his very real experiments in conjuring, sorcery, alchemy, and magical-sexual rituals (carried out with who knows whom!), but it may have also been a way to conceal his work in cryptography and ciphers (the Enochian alphabet and language being perhaps above all a way of encrypting messages using a secret code).

## Assessing John Dee

How, ultimately, do we assess John Dee? Was he delusional in terms of believing in angelic conversations and magic? Harshly, Shumaker agrees with Luigi Firpo[107] concerning "the downfall of his [Dee's] mind and investigative methods after his meeting with Kelly [Kelley] in 1582."[108] Of course, this may have never occurred in a literal sense if Edward Kelley did not really exist, at least not as Dee describes him. Still, Shumaker's point is clear. Shumaker and like-minded thinkers would…

> …pass a decisively negative judgment upon the whole later part of his [Dee's] career [i.e., the period of his séances and so forth] and to condemn, along with the angelic conversations, the recurrent tendency of mankind to find shortcuts, through all the varieties of magic, to the reliable knowledge about humanity and the universe toward which men may legitimately aspire… To this judgment may be added the impossibility that information of the kind obtained by Dee in the séances could ever, no matter how copiously elaborated, add up to 'science'.[109]

This is a very harsh assessment indeed, but also contains some basic assumptions on the part of Shumaker that may not be true. It is true that Dee became disillusioned with his purely "academic" and "scientific" studies, writing...

> All my life time I had spent in learning: but for this forty years continually, in sundry manners, and in divers Countries, with great pain, care, and cost, I had from degree to degree sought to come by the best knowledge that man might attain unto in the world: and I found (at length) that neither any man living, nor any Book I could yet meet withal, was able to teach me those truths I desired and longed for .[110]

Long before becoming involved in séances, Dee had criticized common astronomers who "suffered under the open sky"[111] when they could gain certain types of information from ancient signs and symbols. However, this does not mean that Dee completely gave up his more conventional studies (and indeed there is plenty of evidence that he did not, and he viewed scrying using a crystal or mirror as an expanded form of optics, a not uncommon idea among his contemporaries), but rather he began to supplement his studies with what we might refer to as more spiritual, mystical, and revelatory undertakings. Certainly Dee is not the only scientist or scholar to have found his conventional academic studies less than complete, and thus turned to other types of evidence in order to expand them and increase a holistic understanding of the world and cosmos. Furthermore, contra Shumaker's assertions, it is not at all clear that Dee was taking a shortcut to knowledge with his "angelic conversations". Rather, he spent some three to four decades pursuing his studies along these lines. He kept meticulous notes, questioned the results of the séances, repeated the "experiments", and so on. Dee approached the séances as any good scientist of the time might approach a series of experiments.[112] In modern terms, I would argue that Dee was pursuing serious studies in parapsychology and psychical research.

**Robert M. Schoch** received his Ph.D. in Geology and Geophysics from Yale University, and since 1984 has been a full-time faculty member at the College of General Studies of Boston University. The author of numerous works, his most recent book is *Forgotten Civilization: The Role of Solar Outbursts in Our Past and Future* (Inner Traditions, 2012). Dr. Schoch's personal website is www.robertschoch.com.

# Science and

"Few men have imagination enough for the truth of reality." - Goethe

by *Ray Grasse*

During the last few hundred years our understanding of the universe has been transformed in profound ways by the advent of scientific thought. Displacing the religious and mythological notions that shaped our perceptions for millennia, we found ourselves encountering a new pantheon of material laws and principles dramatically different from those of earlier times. Relativity theory, quantum mechanics, entanglement, the quark, the laws of thermodynamics – these are just a few of the unusual new concepts that have come to populate the imaginal landscape of contemporary thought.

But might there be a deeper significance to this process of scientific discovery than generally realized? Do these varied findings describe for us the hard facts of an outer physical world, or of an inner, psychological one? In fact, as we're about to see, the truth may actually involve a bit of both.

## Science as Symbol

We tend to regard science as being a dispassionate search for truth which utilizes the methods of experimentation, deduction, and rational analysis as its primary tools. In this way, scientists have diligently sought to uncover the laws of nature as they actually exist in the world "out there," unfiltered by human bias or emotion.

Yet there is reason to believe that what we're witnessing in the progress of science throughout the centuries has been as much a reflection of inner, psychological exploration, projected out onto the world, as it is one of external discovery. That's not to say science is "nothing more" than a psychological construct with no objective relevance or reality, simply that the relationship between these two spheres, outer and inner, may be more intimate and complex than generally realized. Said a bit differently, it's possible that the human imagination mirrors the world around it in ways that allow it to grasp those natural principles and laws commensurate with its own level of insight and understanding.

One need only examine the history of scientific breakthroughs through the centuries in relation to our shifting cultural values to notice the curious similarity that's always existed between these two. Consider the way that just as "relativity" began emerging in the sciences we find much the same principle emerging in other fields, too, from the visual relativism of cubist art to the narrative relativism of James Joyce's novels, to the cultural relativism proposed by anthropologists.

Or, consider how just as our material universe was being decentralized by Copernicus, who dethroned the Sun as the center of our solar system, our religious universe was also being "decentralized" as Luther and the Protestant Reformation began loosening the grip of Catholicism on Western society.

Understood this way, the ongoing history of scientific inquiry begins to appear less like a succession of hard facts about the objective world than as a series of mirrors to shifts in the human imagination. As the pioneer physicist Werner Heisenberg, father of the "uncertainty principle," put it:

> (We have seen) that the changes in the foundation of modern science may perhaps be viewed as symptoms of shifts in the fundamentals of our existence, when then express themselves simultaneously in many places, be it changes in our way of life or our usual thoughts forms, be it in external catastrophes, wars, or revolutions.[1]

With this as a starting point, I'd like to briefly explore some other correspondences that have occurred between emerging scientific ideas and changes in society. In particular, I'd like to turn our attention to the some of the major stages in our shifting views of the atom. Perhaps more than any other, it's this basic concept that has shaped the course of modern science. As the essential building block of nature, it's only natural to look toward this image as the ideal screen on which to find the changing projections of our unfolding self-knowledge. As the basic unit of the world, the atom serves as a perfect analog for that basic unit of human social experience: the individual psyche. In this way, the history of the atom reveals itself to be a mirror to nothing less than the unfolding history of the modern Western ego.

## THE ORIGINS OF ATOMIC THEORY

The search for the origins of modern atomic theory takes us back to the time of ancient Greece, to the world of Democritus and Leucippus

– the same general period as the origins of modern individualism and psychological thought. For just as Democritus was suggesting that the universe could be resolved into the existence of indivisible particles, so Greek political philosophy was giving birth to the revolutionary and psychologically transformative idea that society could be understood in terms of its primary component, the individual (from the Latin *individuus* – meaning "indivisible").

With the decline of Greek philosophy and culture, it would be another two thousand years before the concept of the atom became fully integrated into the corpus of scientific thought, with the rise of the modern scientific method in the $17^{th}$ century. It was then that atomic theory joined hands with the mechanistic worldview suggested by scientists like Newton and Descartes, both of whom likened the interaction between nature's discrete parts to the cause-and-effect interplay of billiard balls on a table.

And so it was during that same period that we find the full-scale re-emergence of individualistic thought as well. As we view the world, so we view ourselves, and during an age when the archetypal building block of nature was increasingly defined in the discrete, analytic terms of the new science, so our view of human personality was becoming increasingly "atomistic" and independent as well, with the emerging belief that each individual's experience represents the fundamental reference point of social reality. Indeed, the mechanistic model that helped scientists understand the interactions of atoms also served as a model for social theorists like Thomas Hobbes and John Locke (one of the founding figures of modern democracy), who used it to help explain the behavior of human society. Just as the actions of a gas cloud could be understood in terms of the interaction between its essential atomic or molecular components, Locke believed that the economic and political patterns of a society could likewise be understood through an analysis of its individual members.[2]

## Opening the Atom

Perhaps the single most dramatic change in our understanding of the atom came during the late 19th century, when scientists obtained their first glimpse into its mysterious interior. Prior to this point, most scientists regarded the atom as something fundamental and concrete, nature's "ground floor" beyond which our conceptual tools would likely never penetrate. This appeared so certain that some prominent scientists even suggested we had finally solved most of nature's essential mysteries, and that the only remaining tasks were those of tying up loose ends of existing theories.

Then, with the discovery of the electron by J.J. Thompson in 1897, that longstanding view experienced a seismic shift with the realization that beneath the atom's surface existed another, previously unknown dimension of nature – the "sub-atomic" level of matter. Our visible world was just the proverbial tip of the iceberg, it seemed, beneath which lay an even vaster realm of reality hidden from ordinary view.

At virtually the exact same time, an analogous development was taking place in our understanding of the human psyche as well, with the advent of modern depth psychology and its discovery of the "subconscious mind." Earlier psychologists had largely regarded the conscious personality as, like the atom, indivisible and concrete, and that our waking thoughts and perceptions circumscribed the essential boundaries of everyday experience.

With the publication of Sigmund Freud's *Interpretation of Dreams* in November of 1899, that view was shaken to its core by a theory previously suspected mainly by poets and philosophers – that of a human "subconscious." In this historic volume, Freud argued that beneath the surface of everyday consciousness lie a vast dimension of emotion and thought that was greater than our conscious world of thoughts and feelings, but was largely hidden from view. While difficult to perceive, it was partially visible through such symbolic expressions as nightly dreams or ordinary slips of the tongue. Whereas earlier psychologists had sought to understand human nature in terms of our observable surface behaviors – not unlike the way pre-20th century physicists studied the atom through its observable, quantifiable features – Freud believed the study of human psychology was properly understood only through a deeper understanding of this subconscious domain of experience.[3]

## CONTINUING REVOLUTIONS IN ATOMIC THEORY

During the following decades, the discoveries unfolding in both of these spheres, the sub-atomic and the subconscious, continued to parallel each other in often surprising ways.

At first, a simple "orbital" model was proposed to help explain the atom's structure and behavior. Suggested by Niels Bohr and Ernst Rutherford in 1911, this model depicted the atom as a kind of miniature solar system, with a central nucleus surrounded by orbiting electrons. In psychology this theory became a template for both Freud and his student Carl Jung, who employed the orbital image to illustrate the dynamics of human psychology. But whereas Freud chose to place the ego in the central position corresponding to the atom's nucleus, Jung felt it more accurate to reserve that central point for his key concept of the "self," in turn exiling the ego out to the psyche's periphery.

It wasn't long before this simplistic model gave way to more complex understandings on both fronts. Having stepped into the vast interior of the atom, physicists found themselves encountering a world of unprecedented strangeness that resembled nothing so much as Lewis Carroll's tale of Alice adventure through the looking glass. Here were particles that seemed capable of traveling both forwards and backwards in time, which could be in two places at once, or that might exist only as "probabilities." At this deeper level of matter, scientists encountered laws and characteristics that seemed to defy the orderly logic of everyday, macroscopic physics.

In the realm of psychology, researchers were arriving at conclusions almost as unusual as those emerging in science. Here, too, was a dimension of experience where the prevailing laws seemed more akin to those of dream logic than the linear characteristics of daily rationality. An especially graphic expression of that shift was visible in the works of artists and writers who were deeply influenced by the unfolding developments in psychology, such as surrealist painters like Salvador Dali, Rene Magritte, and Max Ernst, or novelists like James Joyce, all of whom strove to give expression to the subtleties of the unconscious mind. In works like Joyce's *Ulysses* and *Finnegans Wake*, for instance, we encounter a world of mythic resonances and dizzying correspondences that would seem perfectly at home in the newly emerging "zoo" of quantum physics. Indeed, there's something fitting about the fact that the name chosen to designate one of subatomic physics' most important particles – the quark – was drawn directly from the pages of *Finnegans Wake*!

## The Holistic Atom

Among the new discoveries about the atom was the surprising insight that it might be best understood not as an isolated "thing" so much as a complex web of relations. According to quantum physics, the physical world itself must be seen…

> …not (as) a structure built out of independently existing unanalyzable entities, but rather a web of relationships between elements whose meanings arise wholly from their relationships to the whole.[4]

In psychology, theorists like Harry Stack Sullivan were proposing a similarly "holistic" view of human nature, with the suggestion that personality is best understood not in isolation but as inseparably entwined within the web of social relationships it partakes in. Likewise, Carl Jung increasingly came to perceive the human personality as playing host to a dynamically interacting array of "complexes" and archetypal patterns. He further believed, with his theory of the collective unconscious, that the psychic roots of each person were fundamentally entwined with those of all beings.

Carl Jung

No less revolutionary in the realm of science was the disturbing element of "unpredictability" that characterized the behavior of particles at the smallest levels. In direct contrast to the secure determinism of macroscopic, everyday phenomena, physicists discovered that the more closely one examined the atom's interior, the less it lent itself to predictable analysis. At the level of sub-atomic matter, nature itself almost seemed to be ruled by chance. As unpredictable as things appeared at the level of *individual* atoms, though, scientists learned that by examining atoms in *large numbers* they could establish a statistical curve which made accurate predictions possible. The larger the number of atoms, it turned out, the more accurate one's predictions could be.

On a cultural level, that element of unpredictability was paralleled by the rise of an analogous view in our understanding of human behavior. While the actions of any one individual might be unpredictable, when analyzed in large enough numbers it was possible to predict behavioral patterns with great accuracy – an insight that held particular appeal for proponents of Marxist thought, with their emphasis on quantity over quality. As the philosopher Immanuel Kant remarked long ago, while each lover may see their relationship as unique and all-encompassing, the man down at the registry office somehow knows there will be more marriages in Spring than in Winter!

## Exploiting the Energies of the Atom

As important as these various developments were, they were superceded by an even more far-reaching development: the unlocking of the massive energies contained within the atom. This began with the first successful splitting of the atom in 1933, and came to its fiery climax with the detonation of the first atomic bomb in 1945. As Carl Jung suggested, we can look to this historical development as a profound symbol for humankind's awakening to the enormous powers housed within the human psyche itself – energies that could be employed towards either constructive or destructive ends.

Curiously, 1933 was also the year Adolf Hitler began his ascent to power as Chancellor of Germany, a development that likewise came to its apocalyptic climax in 1945 with Hitler's death (and subsequent incineration). It's easy to see in the figure of Hitler an extraordinary – if terrifying – example of the human mind's ability to draw upon the latent energies of the psyche. From the standpoint of the ego, Hitler's rise to power was indeed a "triumph of the will," to borrow Leni Reifenstahl's famed phrase; but it was a sort of will wedded to the darkest instinctual energies of the human psyche. Some of those attending Hitler's speeches remarked on the nearly hypnotic power he seemed to exert on listeners, as though he were channeling a force larger than himself, one rooted in the depths of the European psyche. Hitler's political masterstroke seems to have been his realization that the secret of mass influence lay not in well-reasoned arguments, as many politicians believed, but through appealing to the primal impulses of the human psyche. Towards that end, Hitler and his associates often employed mythic and religious elements in Nazi ceremonies and iconography towards manipulating public opinion.

Carrying this analogy one step further, we find yet another correspondence in the scientific principle of the "chain reaction," whereby energies released from a single atom can catalyze the release of energies contained within many adjoining atoms. This offers an apt metaphor for the way certain charismatic individuals like Hitler, Mussolini or Hirohito, or even Churchill and Roosevelt, were able to ignite the passions of fellow men and women towards effecting profound social change, towards either good or ill.

## New Directions

Since the time of Hiroshima and Nagasaki, scientists have continued deepening their knowledge of the atom, and in the process have expanded the list of sub-atomic particles from the roughly two-dozen known by the end of World War II to the hundreds of nuclear particles and anti-particles now officially recognized by physicists.

Among the more intriguing (and speculative) developments resulting from this exploration has been what some call the "Many Worlds" hypothesis, which suggests an endlessly proliferating number of worlds out of the probabilities described by quantum mechanics. Then there is the hotly debated notion of "superstrings," with its proposed ten dimensions of reality, as well as Alan Guth's theory of the "inflationary universe" with its notion of multiple universes emerging out of the Big Bang. Any one of these theories, if confirmed, would represent a revolutionary development in the progression of science; but what could they possibly mean as mirrors to shifts in our understanding of the human mind? One possibility might be found in the research of figures like Russell Targ, Hal Putoff, and Dean Radin into the realm of psychic and "paranormal" phenomena, and the hidden powers of human consciousness. We may be standing on the threshold of a dramatically new view of our world, both inwardly and outwardly.

And what of scientific discovery over the next 50, 100, or even 10,000 years? In a curious echo of the late 19th century, we once again hear some scientists optimistically proclaim that we could be on the verge of solving nearly all of nature's essential secrets, and perhaps even creating an all-encompassing "theory of everything."

Yet if scientific discovery is as much an inner process of exploration as an outer one, then one has to wonder whether there can ever truly be an "end" to our explorations; for if the limits of our science closely mirror those of our imagination, then our grasp of the external universe will come to an end only when we've ceased plumbing the fathomless depths of the human psyche.

> **Ray Grasse** is a writer, photographer, and musician living in Illinois. He worked for ten years on the editorial staffs of Quest Books and *The Quest* magazine, and is author of *The Waking Dream: Unlocking the Symbolic Language of Our Lives*, and *Signs of the Times: Unlocking the Symbolic Language of World Events*. His website is www.raygrasse.com.

# ENDNOTES

## *Greg Taylor - The Uninvited (p. 45)*

Acknowledgements:

As a large portion of the reports and testimony in this particular case were published in Icelandic, this article relies heavily on translations and information presented in the wonderful monograph "The Icelandic Physical Medium Indridi Indridason", by Loftur R. Gissurarson and Erlendur Haraldsson (*Proceedings of the Society for Psychical Research* Vol. 57, Part 214, January 1989), and *Icelandic Spiritualism*, by Loftur Reimar Gissurarson and William H. Swatos, Jr. For more detailed presentations on this case I encourage the interested reader to consult these sources. The former also features a bibliography of the original source documents for further research.

Notes:

1. Please note that the séance presented at the beginning of the essay is a fictionalized version for presentation purposes. However, it was created by combining testimony and accounts from a number of Indridason's actual seances. The phenomena presented all happened at some stage in his mediumship, though they may not have all happened as presented at one particular séance.

## *Richard Andrews - Herne the Hunter (p. 89)*

Notes:

1. Ainsworth, William Harrison (1843) *Windsor Castle: An Historical Romance*. Henry Colburn.

2. Fitch, Eric (1994) *In Search of Herne the Hunter*. Capall Bann.
3. Cooper, J.C. (1979) *An Illustrated encyclopaedia of Traditional Symbols*. Thames and Hudson.
4. Bromwich, Rachel (1960) 'Celtic Dynastic Themes and the Breton Lays', *Etudes Celtiques*, 9, 439-74.
5. Grenham, John (1993) *Clans and Families of Ireland*. Gill & Macmillan.
6. Matthews, Caitlin (1989) *Arthur and the Sovereignty of Britain*. Arkana.
7. Frazer, James (1998) *The Golden Bough: A Study in Magic and Religion - A New Abridgement from the Second and Third Editions*. Oxford World's Classics.
8. Murray, Margaret (1954) *The Divine King in England*. Faber and Faber.
9. Stevens, Phil (1996) *Medieval Surrey Heath*. Surrey Heath Local History Club.
10. Graves, Robert (1984) *Greek Myths - Illustrated Edition*. Penguin Books.

*Jason Colavito - The Origin of the Space Gods (p. 129)*

Acknowledgements:

This article contains some material that originally appeared in "Charioteer of the Gods," *Skeptic* 10.4 (2004).

Notes:

1. Kenneth L. Feder, "Skeptics, Fence-Sitters, and True Believers: Student Acceptance of an Improbable Prehistory," in Garrett G. Fagan (ed.), *Archaeological Fantasies* (New York: Routledge, 2006), 78.
2. H. P. Lovecraft, "The Call of Cthulhu," in *The Fiction* (New York: Barnes & Noble, 2008), 367.
3. H. P. Lovecraft, *At the Mountains of Madness*, in *The Fiction*, 769.
4. Ibid., 771.
5. Helena Blavatsky, *The Secret Doctrine*, Vol. 2: Anthropogenesis (Point Loma, California: The Aryan Theosophical Press, 1917), 115.
6. W. Scott-Elliot, *The Lost Lemuria* (London: Theosophical Publishing Society, 1904), 34-44.
7. Ibid., 36.
8. Charles Fort, *The Book of the Damned* (New York: Boni and Liveright, 1919), 66.
9. Ibid., 118, 124, 164.

10. Ibid., 164.
11. Scott Roxborough, "Ridley Scott, Michael Fassbender, Noomi Rapace Tease 'Prometheus' at CineEurope," *The Hollywood Reporter*, June 28, 2011 <http://www.hollywoodreporter.com/news/ridley-scott-michael-fassbender-noomi-206321>.
12. Jason Colavito, *The Cult of Alien Gods: H. P. Lovecraft and Extraterrestrial Pop Culture* (Prometheus, 2005).
13. Richard L. Tierney, "Cthulhu in Mesoamerica," *Crypt of Cthulhu* no. 9 (1981).
14. Robert M. Price and Charles Garofalo, "Chariots of the Old Ones?", in Robert M. Price (ed.), *Black, Forbidden Things: Cryptical Secrets from the "Crypt of Cthulhu"* (Mercer Island, WA: Starmont House, 1992), 86-87.

## Theo Paijmans - Hermann Göring and The Edelweiss Society (p. 151)

Notes:

1. A documentary film on Count Eric von Rosen directed by his grandson Peter Nestler, *Tod und Teufel*, was released in 2009.
2. Having accidentally shot the mother bear on a trip to Finnish Karelia, he took two cubs with him. One survived. http://www.rockelstad.se/english/legends.asp
3. http://www.rockelstad.se/english/hermann-goring.asp
4. Anna Maria Siegmund, *Die Frauen der Nazis*, Ueberreuter, 1998, pages 23-24.
5. http://www.rockelstad.se/english/legends.asp
6. Anna Maria Siegmund, *Die Frauen der Nazis*, Ueberreuter, 1998, page 25.
7. http://www.rockelstad.se/english/hermann-goring.asp
8. Much has been written on the origin and evolution of the swastika before it became the symbol of the NSDAP and how it entered Nazism. See for instance the most recent study by David Luhrssen, *Hammer of the Gods, the Thule Society and the Birth of Nazism*, Potomac Books, 2012, pages 188-189.
9. Anna Maria Siegmund, *Die Frauen der Nazis*, Ueberreuter, 1998, page 25.
10. Werner Gerson, *Le Nazisme Scocieté Secrete*, Productions de Paris, 1969, Chapter XVII: Edelweiss, pages 281-298.
11. http://en.wikipedia.org/wiki/Mary_von_Rosen
12. Anna Maria Siegmund, *Die Frauen der Nazis*, Ueberreuter, 1998, pages 27-28.
13. David Irving, *Göring A Biography*, 2002, page 43.
14. Fanny Gräfin von Wilamowitz-Moellendorff, *Carin Göring*, Martin Warneck verlag, 1938, 1943, pages 7, 13.

15. Anna Maria Siegmund, *Die Frauen der Nazis*, Ueberreuter, 1998, pages 26-27.
16. Fanny Gräfin von Wilamowitz-Moellendorff, *Carin Göring*, Martin Warneck verlag, 1938, 1943, pages 7, 13.
17. See for instance the article 'Huldine Beamish, född Mosander. ("Edelweiss"), in *Idun, Praktisk Veckotidning för Kvinnan och Hemmet*, 20 January 1893.
18. Edelweiss, *Spiritism*, John Lovell Company, 1891.
19. Veit Loers, *Okkultismus und Avantgarde: von Munch bis Mondrian*, Edition Tertium, 1895, page 114.
20. Rev. Prof. G. Henslow, *The Proofs of the Truths of Spritiualism*, Kegan Paul, Trench, Trübner & Co. Ltd., 1919, page 179.
21. Fanny Gräfin von Wilamowitz-Moellendorff, *Carin Göring*, Martin Warneck verlag, 1938, 1943, page 24.
22. See for instance: Tobias Scheidegger, *Mythos Edelweiss: zur Kulturgeschichte eines alpinen Symbols. Eine Dokumentation. Recherchiert und verfasst im Auftrag der Botanischen Gärten Zürich und Genf*, 2008. www.expo-edelweiss.ch
23. Elisabeth Braw Riccini, 'Carin Göring – Nazitysklands svenska ikon', *Popülar Historia*, 2, 2000, http://www.popularhistoria.se/artiklar/carin-goring-nazitysklands-svenska-ikon/
24. http://www.rockelstad.se/historia/maryssb.asp
25. Elisabeth Braw Riccini, 'Carin Göring – Nazitysklands svenska ikon', *Popülar Historia*, 2, 2000, http://www.popularhistoria.se/artiklar/carin-goring-nazitysklands-svenska-ikon/
26. First published in Fanny Gräfin von Wilamowitz-Moellendorff, *Carin Göring*, Martin Warneck verlag, 1938, also quoted in Werner Gerson, *Le Nazisme Societé Secrete*, Productions de Paris, 1969, page 288.
27. See: Theo Paijmans, *Free Energy Pioneer: John Worrell Keely*, IllumiNet Press 1998, AUP 2004.
28. Henry Stevens, *Hitler's Suppressed and Still-Secret Weapons, Science and Technology*, AUP, 2007, pages 209-211.

## Paolo Sammut - *The Starry Wisdom* (p. 169)

Notes:

1. Pertaining of information, contacts and concepts which originate from "elsewhere" and enter sphere of human consciousness via the unconsciousness.
2. The word *sidereal* is here used to describe how a particular perspective is needed

when looking at some of the characterise and concepts which Grant describes.
3. Kenneth Grant, *Outer Gateways*, Skoob books, 1994
4. Arthur Machen, *The Great God Pan*, John Lane, 1984
5. John Keel, *The Mothman Prophecies*, Panther Books, 1975
6. Daniel Harms and John Wisdom Gonce, *The Necronomicon Files*, Red Wheel/Weiser, 2003
7. Kenneth Grant, *Outer Gateways*, Skoob Publishing, 1994, pp5
8. Kenneth Grant, *The Magical Revival*, Muller, 1971
9. Technically speaking gematria is the process of assigning numbers to meaningful words and then looking at words with the same number to find meaningful connections. Kenneth Grant expands upon this with creative gematria which takes things further as we shall see later.
10. Interestingly this suggests that the word may be Enochian in nature.
11. Kenneth Grant, *Gamaliel: The diary of a Vampire & Dance*, Doll Dance, Starfire, 2003.
12. Although the idea of a vampire as a life-force hungry ghost is very important and crops up frequently in folklore and the occult.
13. Dion Fortune, *Moon Magic*, Red Wheel/Weiser, 2003.
14. Tera. See Bram Stokers *Jewel of the Seven Stars*.
15. Kenneth Grant, *The Ninth Arch*, Starfire Publishing, 2002, pp386
16. In Stoker, she is called Tera as a pun on Margaret, the female protagonist in the tale. Tera is of course the last four letters of Margaret.
17. Such as *Awakening* (1980) and *Legend of the Mummy* (1997)
18. We find with this story echoes Aleister Crowley's tale *The Dream Circean* which is itself a retelling of an older tale about a person visiting and being entertained within a house, only to find a short while later that it has been boarded up for years.
19. Kenneth Grant, *Hecate's Fountain*, Skoob, 1992
20. Alan Moore, "Beyond Our Ken", http://www.fulgur.co.uk/authors/grant/articles/beyond-our-ken/
21. Dieckmann and starring Max Schreck, *Nosferatu*, 1922
22. Kenneth Grant, *Hecate's Fountain*, Skoob Publishing, 1992, pp53
23. Kenneth Grant, *Hecate's Fountain*, Skoob Publishing, 1992, pp10
24. Kenneth Grant, *Zos Speaks*, Fulgur Publishing, 1999.
25. Kenneth Grant, *Images and Oracles of Austin Osman Spare*, Muller, 1975.
26. Michael Bertiaux, *The Voudon Gnostic Workbook*, Red Wheel/Weiser, 2007
27. Andrew D. Chumbley, *Azoëtia*, Xoanon, 1992, 2002
28. Alan Moore, "Beyond Our Ken", http://www.fulgur.co.uk/authors/grant/articles/

beyond-our-ken/
29. English Heretic, *Tales of the New Isis Lodge*, 2009. http://www.english-heretic.org.uk/
30. Universal Studios, *The Mummy*, 1932
31. HP Lovecraft, *Fungi From Yuggoth*, Various, 1929 to 1930
32. *Invasion of the Body Snatchers*, 1956
33. Kenneth Grant, *Grist to Whose Mi*ll, Starfire Publishing, 2012

*Ian 'Cat' Vincent - Killing Slenderman (p. 185)*

Acknowledgements:

Huge thanks to all the Slenderman creators and commenters – especially those at *Slenderbloggins, Encyclopedia Slenderia* and the Tumblrblog *Fuck Yeah Slenderman*. No wifin!

Notes:

As with my first Slenderman article, a page with links and annotations can be found on my blog at www.catvincent.com.

*Robert M. Schoch - The Enigmatic Doctor Dee (p. 211)*

Bibliography:

Calder, I. R. F. *John Dee: Studied as an English Neoplatonist*. Ph.D. dissertation, University of London, 1952 (Available from http://www.johndee.org/calder/html/TOC.html Accessed 1 September 2012).
Casaubon, Meric. *A True and Faithful Relation of what passed for many years between Dr. John Dee . . . and some Spirits*. London: T. Garthwait, 1659.
Conway, David. *Secret Wisdom: The Occult Universe Revealed*. London: Vega, 2002.
de Vesme, Caesar. *A History of Experimental Spiritualism*. Vol. 1, *Primitive Man* (translated from the French by Stanley de Brath). Vol. 2, *Peoples of Antiquity*

(translated from the French by Fred Rothwell). London: Rider and Company, 1931.

Deacon, Richard. *John Dee: Scientist, Geographer, Astrologer and Secret Agent to Elizabeth I*. London: Frederick Muller, 1968.

Dee, John. *Monas Hieroglyphica*. Antwerp: Willem Silvius, 1564.

della Riviera, Cesare. *Il Mondo Magico de gli Heroi*. Milano: Pietro Martire Locarni, 1605.

di Sospiro, Guido Mina, and Joscelyn Godwin. *The Forbidden Book*. New York: The Disinformation Company, 2012.

Evans, R. J. W. *Rudolf II and His World: A Study in Intellectual History, 1576 – 1612*. Oxford: Clarendon Press, 1973.

Evola, Julius. *The Hermetic Tradition: Symbols and Teachings of the Royal Art*. Rochester, Vermont: Inner Traditions, 1995 (originally published in Italian in 1931 as *Le Tradizione Ermetica*).

Fell Smith, Charlotte. *John Dee (1527-1608)*. London: Constable and Company, 1909.

Firpo, Luigi. "John Dee, Scienziato, Negromante e Avventuriero." *Rinascimento* III (1952) [quoted in, and cited from, Shumaker, 1982].

Forshaw, Peter J. "The Early Alchemical Reception of John Dee's *Monas Hieroglyphica*." *Ambix*, vol. 52, no. 3, pp. 247-269 (November 2005).

French, Peter J. *John Dee: The World of an Elizabethan Magus*. London: Routledge and Kegan Paul, 1972.

Gattey, Charles Nielson. *Visionaries and Seers: They Saw Tomorrow*. Bridport, Dorset: Prism, 1977 (reprint, 1988).

Hamilton Jones, J. W., translator, *The Hieroglyphic Monad* by John Dee. London: John M. Watkins, 1947.

Lévi, Éliphas [Alphonse Louis Constant]. *Transcendental Magic: Its Doctrine and Ritual* (translated by Arthur Edward Waite). York Beach, Maine: Weiser Books, 2001 (originally published in French in two volumes, *Dogme et Rituel de la Haute Magie*, Germer Baillière, Paris, 1856, second edition 1861).

Lévi, Éliphas [Alphonse Louis Constant]. *Magic: A History of Its Rites, Rituals and Mysteries* (translated by Arthur Edward Waite). Mineola, New York: Dover Publications 2006 (originally published as *Histoire de la magie avec une exposition claire et précise de la magie, de ses procédés, de ses rites et de ses mystères*, Germer Baillière, Paris, 1860).

Norvill, Roy. *The Language of the Gods*. Bath, Avon, U.K.: Ashgrove Press, 1987.

Schoch, Robert M., and Logan Yonavjak, editors and compilers. *The Parapsychology Revolution: A Concise Anthology of Paranormal and Psychical Research*. New York: Jeremy P. Tarcher/Penguin, 2008.

Shumaker, Wayne. *Renaissance Curiosa: John Dee's Conversations with Angels, Girolamo Cardano's Horoscope of Christ, Johannes Trithemius and Cryptography, George Dalgarno's Universal Language.* Temple, Arizona: Arizona Center for Medieval and Renaissance Studies, 1982 (reprint, 2003).

Szőnyi, György E. *John Dee's Occultism: Magical Exaltation through Powerful Signs.* Albany, New York: State University of New York Press, 2004.

Tyson, Donald. *Enochian Magic for Beginners: The Original System of Angel Magic.* St. Paul, Minnesota: Llewellyn, 1997.

Zetterberg, J. Peter. "John Dee's Celestial Egg." *Isis*, vol. 70, no. 3, pp. 385-392 (September 1979).

**Notes:**

1. Deacon, 1968, p. 13.
2. Deacon, 1968, p. 23.
3. Where he spent time later in his life; Shumaker, 1982, p. 50, footnote 3, citing R. J. W. Evans, 1973.
4. Deacon, 1968.
5. Description by William Aubrey, who knew Dee, quoted by Gattey, 1977, p. 82.
6. Deacon, 1968, pp. 106-107.
7. Szőnyi, 2004, p. 185.
8. Deacon, 1968, p. 55.
9. French, 1972, p. 36.
10. Shumaker, 1982, p. 93.
11. Shumaker, 1982, p. 9.
12. Shumaker, 1982, p. 96.
13. Calder, 1952, chapter 6.
14. Calder, 1952, chapter 6.
15. Deacon, 1968, pp. 56; italics in the original.
16. E.g., Shumaker, 1982.
17. With many encoded "conjurations", cabbalistic permutations, and phrases, not perhaps unlike those found in della Riviera, 1605; see also di Sospiro and Godwin, 2012.
18. Szőnyi, 2004, p. 107; see also Deacon 1968, p. 57.
19. Schoch and Yonavjak, 2008.
20. Deacon, 1968, p. 59; Shumaker, 1982, p. 16; Szőnyi, 2004, p. 161.
21. See French, 1972, pp. 62-63.

22. Szőnyi, 2004, p. 169.
23. Szőnyi, 2004, p. 162.
24. Shumaker, 1982, pp. 16-17.
25. Shumaker, 1982, p. 11.
26. Zetterberg, 1979, p. 386.
27. Szőnyi, 2004, pp. 157-159.
28. Szőnyi, 2004, p. 171.
29. Thomas Tymme, circa 1610, who planned but did not complete an English translation of *Monas Hieroglyphica*; quoted by Szőnyi, 2004, p. 171.
30. French, 1972, p. 79.
31. Theorem XXI, Hamilton Jones, 1947, p. 34, italics in the original.
32. Forshaw, 2005, pp. 256-257.
33. Szőnyi 2004, p. 168.
34. Szőnyi 2004, pp. 168-169.
35. As Trithemius asserted concerning the power of numbers and talismanic devices; see Forshaw, 2005, p. 149.
36. Szőnyi, 2004, p. 169, italics in the original.
37. Cf. della Riviera, 1605.
38. Deacon, 1968, p. 5.
39. See Lévi, 2001, pp. 186, 307-310.
40. Forshaw, 2005, p. 258.
41. Deacon, 1968, p. 125.
42. Deacon, 1968, pp. 160-165.
43. della Riviera, 1605, p. 24; Evola, 1995.
44. Forshaw, 2005, p. 257.
45. Forshaw, 2005.
46. Evola, 1995, p. 82.
47. As it is referred to in Lévi, 2001, p. 12; see also Lévi, 2006, p. 211, footnote 2.
48. Evola, 1995, p. 82.
49. Lévi, 2001, p. xiv.
50. Lévi, 2001, p. xv.
51. Evola, 1995, p. 82.
52. Lévi, 2001, p. 12.
53. Evola, 1995, p. 82, italics in the original.
54. Lévi, 2001, p. xv.
55. Evola, 1995, p. 83.

56. Casaubon, 1659.
57. See, for instance, Tyson, 1997.
58. Gattey, 1977, p. 59.
59. See Szőnyi, 2004, p. 183.
60. Szőnyi, 2004, p. 195.
61. Gattey, 1977, p. 70.
62. Conway, 2002, p. 98.
63. See summary and references in Deacon, 1968.
64. Gattey, 1977, p. 72.
65. Szőnyi, 2004, p. 278.
66. Szőnyi, 2004, pp. 220-221.
67. Szőnyi, 2004, p. 253.
68. Deacon, 1968, p. 258.
69. Gattey, 1977, p. 71.
70. Gattey, 1977, p. 73.
71. Gattey, 1977, p. 66.
72. Shumaker, 1982, p. 37.
73. Tyson, 1997, p. 39.
74. Tyson, 1997, p. 5.
75. Szőnyi, 2004, p. 190.
76. Szőnyi, 2004, p. 190.
77. Norvill, 1987, pp. 121-122.
78. Shumaker, 1982, pp. 39-41.
79. Shumaker, 1982, p. 41.
80. Cf. Tyson, 1997, pp. 33-34.
81. Shumaker, 1982, p. 41.
82. Quoted in Tyson, 1997, p. 37.
83. According to Tyson, 1997, p. 43.
84. Tyson, 1997, p. 46.
85. French, 1972, p. 113, footnote 2.
86. Shumaker, 1982, p. 26.
87. French, 1972, p. 113, footnote 2.
88. Deacon, 1968, p. 124. Interestingly, in the portrait of John Dee in the Ashmolean Museum, Dee is shown wearing a black skullcap; see frontispiece to French, 1972.
89. Shumaker, 1982, p. 26, quoting Casaubon.

90. Deacon, 1968, p. 259.
91. French, 1972, p. 113, footnote 2.
92. Deacon, 1968, pp. 124, 131.
93. French, 1972, p. 113, footnote 2; Shumaker, 1982, p. 26; Norvill, 1987, p. 115, states that Kelley died in 1597.
94. Norvill, pp. 122-123.
95. See Deacon, 1968, pp. 63-68; Norvill, 1987, p. 120.
96. Norvill, 1987, p. 123.
97. Norvill, 1987, p. 121.
98. Shumaker, 1982, p. 41.
99. Norvill, 1987, p. 124; Deacon, 1968, pp. 131-132.
100. Deacon, 1968, p. 17.
101. Shumaker, 1982, p. 16.
102. Deacon, 1968, p. 34.
103. Norvill, 1987, p. 124.
104. See Norvill, 1987, p. 123.
105. See Deacon, 1968, p. 62.
106. Norvill, 1987, p. 126.
107. Firpo, 1952.
108. Shumaker, 1982, p. 43.
109. Shumaker, 1982, p. 44.
110. Dee quoted in Casaubon, 1659, as quoted by Szőnyi, 2004, p. 183.
111. Zetterberg, 1979, p. 393, quoting from the *Monas Hieroglyphica*.
112. Very much in the spirit of experimental spiritualism as documented by de Vesme, 1931.

## *Ray Grasse - Science and Imagination (p. 241)*

Notes:

1. Werner Heisenberg, "The Representation of Nature in Contemporary Physics," *Daedalus*, Vol. 87, No. 3, Summer, 1958, p. 101.
2. For a more complete explanation of Locke's theory of the relationship between atomic and social behavior, see Fritjof Capra's *The Turning Point*, Simon and Shuster, New York, 1982, p. 68, 69.

3. Although Freud's *Interpretation of Dreams* was not his first formal statement on the subconscious (nor was he its only proponent; Josef Breuer suggested a similar idea in his book *Hypnotic Theory* back in 1882), it's the work commonly regarded as introducing the concept to a worldwide audience.

4. Henry Stapp, "S-Matrix Interpretation of Quantum Theory," quoted by Gary Zukav in *The Dancing Wu Li Masters*, William Morrow and Company, 1979, p. 72.

CPSIA information can be obtained at www.ICGtesting.com
Printed in the USA
BVOW07s1105120814

362576BV00002B/261/P